The Springer Series on Death and Suicide

ROBERT KASTENBAUM, Ph.D., Series Editor

Alan L. Berman, Ph.D., is a professor of psychology at the American University in Washington, DC, and a psychotherapist in private practice at the Washington Psychological Center. He is a Fellow of the American Psychological Association, a Diplomate in Clinical Psychology (American Board of Professional Psychology), and a member of the American Association of Suicidology, the International Association of Suicide Prevention, and the American Orthopsychiatric Association.

Dr. Berman is a past president (1984–1985) of the American Association of Suicidology (AAS) and chair of the AAS Training Committee. He is the recipient of the AAS's 1982 Shneidman Award for Outstanding Contributions in Research in Suicidology. He also has served on the Board of Directors of the National Committee on Youth Suicide Prevention.

Dr. Berman received his B.A. degree from the Johns Hopkins University and his Ph.D. from the Catholic University of America. He has published over 50 articles and book chapters on suicide and related subjects in the professional literature. He is both a consulting editor and the case conference editor of the journal *Suicide and Life Threatening Behavior.*

Dr. Berman conducts an average of 15 to 20 professional training seminars and workshops annually on topics in suicidology. His primary areas of interest relate to youth suicide (assessment and treatment), suicide prevention, and the use of the psychological autopsy in the determination of suicidal death. He appears frequently on both national and local media speaking on these subjects, has twice testified before the U.S. Congress on legislation related to suicide, and serves as an expert witness in legal cases involving possible malpractice in the treatment of suicidal patients, manner of death determinations in equivocal cases, and other issues related to wrongful death.

SUICIDE PREVENTION

CASE CONSULTATIONS

Alan L. Berman, Ph.D.

Editor

Springer Publishing Company
New York

Springer Publishing Company, Inc.
536 Broadway
New York, NY 10012

90 91 92 93 94 / 5 4 3 2 1

Library of Congress Cataloging-in-Publication Data

Suicide prevention: case consultations / Alan L. Berman, editor.
    p. cm.—(Springer series on death and suicide; 10)
   Includes bibliographical references.
   ISBN 0-8261-7120-6
   1. Suicidal behavior—Treatment—Case studies. 2. Suicide-
-Prevention—Case studies. I. Berman, Alan L. (Alan Lee), 1943–
. II. Series.
   RC569.S9363 1990
   362.2'87—dc20   89-26342
                                                CIP
                                                Rev.

Printed in the United States of America

Contents

Preface

This casebook is based on presentations made at a series of case conferences prepared for the 21st Annual Meeting of the American Association of Suicidology (AAS) in Washington, DC, in April 1988. These programs constituted the first attempts at a model of professional education in suicidology by the AAS. Audience reception and participation were so positive and active that the board of directors of the AAS moved to produce this volume as an archival resource and permanent hard copy for future generations of suicidologists. Acknowledgments and thanks are due to the members of the board and in particular to Dr. Charlotte Sanborn, then president of the AAS, for their support of this project.

The quality of an edited volume rests on the creative products of its contributors. It is not fortuitous that the panel of respondents selected to discuss these cases produced work of such quality. Each was well-known as a expert in his or her particular sphere of work and is capable of articulating both a thoughtful and thought-provoking response to a problem presentation. I am grateful to them for their efforts.

The quality of their responses is in part dependent on the stimulus provided by the material. The more personal glimpses provided by the commentators make this work both dynamic and provocative.

Finally, I owe a thank you to those who attended the in vivo panel presentations and who responded to and with these panelists. I owe an apology for not being able to identify for the reader those whose points are so thoughtfully addressed. The bottom line is that suicide prevention is inherently the business of both the named and unnamed who are concerned with the well-being of others.

Contributors

Alan L. Berman, Ph.D., Editor
Professor of Psychology
American University
Washington, DC

Pamela Cantor, Ph.D.
Lecturer on Psychology
Department of Psychiatry
Harvard Medical School
The Cambridge Hospital
Cambridge, Massachusetts

David Clark, Ph.D.
Director
Center for Suicide Research & Prevention
Rush-Presbyterian-St. Luke's Medical
Center
Chicago, Illinois

Sam Heilig, M.S.W.
Former Executive Director
Los Angeles Suicide Prevention Center
Los Angeles, California

Marc Hertzman, M.D.
Director
Hospital Services,
Department of Psychiatry
George Washington University
Medical Center
Washington, DC

Robert Litman, M.D.
Clinical Professor of Psychiatry
University of California at Los Angeles
Los Angeles, California

John Maltsberger, M.D.
Department of Psychiatry
Massachusetts General Hospital
Boston, Massachusetts

Ronald Maris, Ph.D.
Director
Center for the Study of Suicide
University of South Carolina
Columbia, South Carolina

John Meeks, M.D.
Medical Director
Psychiatric Institute of
Montgomery County
Rockville, Maryland

James Moyer
Vice President
Loss Prevention
Marriott Hotels and Resorts
Bethesda, Maryland

Patrick O'Carroll, M.D., M.P.H.
Acting Chief
Intentional Injuries Section
Epidemiology Branch
Division of Injury Epidemiology and
Control
Centers for Disease Control
Atlanta, Georgia

Seymour Perlin, M.D.
Professor of Psychiatry and Behavioral
Sciences
The George Washington University School
of Medicine
Washington, DC

Benjamin Read
Former Undersecretary of State
Attorney
Washington, DC

Richard Seiden, Ph.D., M.P.H.
Psychological Consultant
The Glendon Association
Los Angeles, CA

Andrew Slaby, M.D., M.P.H.
Chief Psychiatrist
The Regent Hospital
New York, New York

Kim Smith, Ph.D.
Co-Director
The Menninger Clinic of Albuquerque
Albuquerque, New Mexico

Mary Smith
Volunteer Telephone Counselor
Crisis Intervention of Houston
Houston, Texas

Zigfrids Stelmachers, Ph.D.
Chief Clinical Psychologist
Hennepin County Medical Center
Minneapolis, Minnesota

James Wells, Ph.D.
Deputy Director
Central New Hampshire Community
Mental Health Services, Inc.
Concord, New Hampshire

Robert Yufit, Ph.D.
Associate Professor
Northwestern University Medical School
Chicago, Illinois

Introduction

This book is written for those in both mental and public health disciplines that have as their central thesis a concern for human life and well-being. It is intended to serve as a teaching tool for clinicians and paraprofessionals, for public health program and community planners. Most important, this book is dedicated to those who see themselves as suicidologists.

Suicidology is a neologism. It does not define a professional discipline. Rather, it serves as a defining attribute applied to the study of suicide. Suicidologists simply are those who specialize in the study of suicide. They are psychiatrists, social workers, psychologists, and psychiatric nurses. They are also epidemiologists, attorneys, city planners, and concerned laypeople. There is no board certification for the professional suicidologist; there simply is a concern for understanding human behavior, for preventing maladaptation and suffering, and, alternatively, for promoting healthy behavior and meaningful existence.

Those who work "in the trenches" with suicidal individuals, providing direct clinical services, often after the fact of an attempt that might have resulted in death, are frequently the first to promote the idea that suicide can be prevented. Anecdotally, they report the successes of their efforts, seeing meaningful lives being constructed out of the remnants of a near death. It is from this clinical perspective that the broader frame of mental and public health prevention efforts has grown, particularly as commanded by the often public nature of suicidal death.

Why a volume on suicide prevention? The best answer is posed by the sheer weight of numbers. In 1987, at the time of this writing the latest year for which we have official mortality data, suicide ranked as the eighth leading cause of death in the United States. There were, 30,796 certified suicides, an average of 1 suicide every 17 minutes. In the past decade, we can document approximately 300,000 suicide deaths, a number almost universally agreed to be a conservative estimate of the true numbers of self-inflicted, intentional deaths.

We have only estimates, as well, of the numbers of those who attempt suicide and survive. Ratios of attempters to completers range from a low of 4:1 among the elderly to a high of 150:1 among the young, accounting in toto for perhaps over 500,000 attempters annually. Thus, if efforts such as those described in this volume were to promote new initiatives significantly affecting the health and well-being of but 1% of this population of suicidal individuals, more than 5,000 lives each year would be so changed. That is a most compelling reason for this book.

There is no shortage of books on suicide and the suicidal individual. The reader, however, would be hard-pressed to find much in the professional literature on suicide prevention, broadly defined to include both community programming efforts and clinical interventions. This is even more true of the case method model of presentation offered in this volume.

Although the case method has long been used in other fields, notably law and business, I believe this volume is unique to the suicidology literature. Whereas case studies of suicidal individuals are commonly reported and even have been the central focus of prior books (e.g., Niswander, Casey, & Humphrey, 1973), to date no effort has been made to use the case method as a problem-oriented instructional tool to pose strategies of intervention and prevention. Discussants providing commentaries on each of the problem situation cases presented in this book accomplish much more than a furthering of our understanding of the case being addressed. They provide a hands-on, practical list of do's and don'ts, each from individual perspectives chosen to maximize a diversity of approaches and opinions.

Cases selected for presentation to discussants were intended to sample the breadth of suicide prevention and intervention issues while obviously being limited in scope. The overall theme, suicide prevention, has been addressed through six case problems, divided into two sections: Part I presents three cases at a level of both primary and secondary prevention, demanding systemic response on a community level; Part II poses three cases at a level of secondary and tertiary prevention in clinical practice. For each case, three discussants provide commentary, followed by an interactive discussion among the respondents and with unnamed members of a conference audience. These often lively and provocative interchanges allow for greater focus to each of the contributor's more formal presentations and for points of disagreement and elucidation to emerge. As such, the goal of this volume is to present a truly multidisciplinary analysis and collaborative response to help reduce potentially suicidogenic environmental conditions and to improve the quality of clinical interventions and resources available to those in need.

Chapter 1 addresses the relative efficacy of several articulated environmental interventions to the problem of a suicide landmark—a jump site. Benjamin Read, the father of a young woman who died as a result of a suicide jump, is a successful lobbyist for a bridge barrier in

Washington, DC; he addresses his response to the case on the basis of three criteria: cost, aesthetics, and effectiveness. Richard Seiden, who has spent a number of years lobbying without success for suicide barriers on the Golden Gate Bridge in San Francisco, reviews the clinical and empirical data regarding why some sites become landmarks and whether potential suicides, thwarted from using one method or site, will simply shift to another. Both Seiden and Read agree that preventive interventions in the environment will work at least in the short term. Balancing their presentations, James Moyer, a specialist in risk management and building security, brings a functional and practical viewpoint to bear on the problem by addressing a number of alternative strategies of environmental control and safety enhancement. These three perspectives provide an exciting panorama of active steps available to the issue of environmental planning for the public welfare.

Chapter 2 presents a case of contagion, which, as described in the introduction by Patrick O'Carroll, the chair of the Centers for Disease Control's work group on suicide clusters, is an amalgam of several real cluster situations. David Clark's response, also is an amalgam of his two perspectives, that of researcher and clinician. Clark first addresses the question of what defines a cluster and suggests that what is thought to be may not be. He then provides the reader with several specific interventions to manage the potentially negative clinical sequelae to initial events in potential clusters. Both John Meeks' and Pamela Cantor's responses, similarly, are built on the premise of their clinical understanding of adolescence and their experience in dealing with cluster intervention situations. It is perhaps remarkable to note the unanimity in the responses of these three panelists. Among several common proposals, each notes the need for predeveloped "game plans," that several target groups must be given immediate and clinical attention, and that the media should be prepared to be part of the solution to, rather than the problem of, suicide clusters.

Chapter 3 presents a problem of secondary intervention at the level of community services, a crisis case presented by telephone to a volunteer-staffed crisis intervention service. Respondents to this case include a director of a crisis service, Zigfrids Stelmachers; a volunteer telephone counselor at a crisis service, Mary Smith; and the former chief certification examiner of the AAS, James Wells, who co-developed standards for service for crisis centers. Thus, three diverse perspectives are evident in approaching a case autopsy of a failed intervention with the result that a large number of specific systemic safeguards and procedural issues are addressed.

Issues of intervention and prevention from the perspective of the mental health practitioner in direct clinical service to patients are addressed in the final three cases. In Chapter 4 an unusual case of a suicide pact is presented and responded to by three senior clinicians. Andrew Slaby autopsies this case with consideration to the biological, psychological, social, and existential issues posed by seriously disturbed patients. Kim Smith brings his profound understanding of the borderline character, or characters, to focus on the different treatment issues presented by such patients. Marc Hertzman differentiates the ethical from the legal considerations that, he argues, are inherent in taking a therapeutic stance with patients with whom we adopt a legal imperative to protect from their own self-destructive urges.

In Chapter 5, a more microtherapeutic issue is posed by a procedural question, that of acquiescing to a suicidal patient's demand to have access to a lethal weapon. As in the discussion of clusters, there is remarkable uniformity in the response of the clinician-consultants: John Maltsberger, a psychiatrist from the East Coast; Sam Heilig, a social worker from the West Coast; and Robert Yufit, a psychologist from the Midwest. Given the opportunity for diversity in their responses, the concordance arrived at in their evaluation of this patient's risk and in the strategies of response proposed suggests that perhaps we are considerably developed in our understanding of these patients and in what we believe works in their treatment.

Finally, Chapter 6 presents a case of treatment failure, one alleging malpractice on the part of those entrusted as caregivers. Three seasoned "expert witnesses," presented an alleged fact outline from the perspective of the plaintiff, are asked to give their opinion on the quality of care given the patient relative to standards opined in their testimonies. Seymour Perlin succinctly addresses issues of inpatient and outpatient management and caregiver attitudes. Ronald Maris, similarly but in greater depth, reviews the variety of considerations that comprise reasonable and prudent care; and Robert Litman frames his approach to the case through the phenomenological lens of the expert witness, giving a unique insight into courtroom and depositional procedures. Among a number of recommendations, he stresses for the clinician the singular importance of documenting clinical decisions and observations with awareness of the potential for legal action in the event of the death of a suicidal patient. Such attention to what we do can only result in more considered and thoughtful approaches to patient treatment. Thus, failures in treatment often become our best teachers, resulting in greater successes in treatment of future patients.

REFERENCE

Niswander, G. D., Casey, T. M., & Humphrey, J.A. (1973). *A panorama of suicide.* Springfield, IL: Charles C Thomas.

I
Suicide Prevention in the Community

1

Suicide Prevention in Public Places

Jumping from a high place accounts for slightly under 1,000 suicidal deaths annually in the United States. An almost equivalent number of accidental falls from high places are recorded each year (Berman, Litman, & Diller, 1989). Although not one of the more common forms of suicidal death in the United States (Salmons, 1984), Great Britain (Sims & O'Brien, 1979) or Australia (Pounder, 1985), jumps from significant height, as public events, attract a great deal of notice and media attention. Thus, they may gain significance as models for imitative behavior. More important, they may be among the most preventable of suicidal behaviors.

But, little is known about this type of fatal injury behavior. Certification of these deaths rests almost exclusively on site investigation data and rarely on investigation of the personal characteristics of the decedent, in spite of evidence that in some cases fatal falls classified as accidents may be disguised suicides (cf., Krueger & Hutcherson, 1978).

We do know that the majority (2/3) of those who jump from heights are male, although non-fatal jumps appear equally divided by sex; jumpers usually are under age 35 and suffering from serious psychiatric disturbance (schizophrenic and/or mood disorders). The major consequences of the method suggest that both intention to die and a desire for attention are primary motives for this type of suicidal person. Jumping from a height of several stories carries a high probability of death or severe mutilative injury, and as it is almost necessarily a public behavior, it often attracts media attention. In a significant minority of non-fatal incidents, jumpers report acting in response to command hallucinations (e.g., voices ordering them to throw themselves out of windows) or delusions (e.g., believing they can fly and attempting to do so) (Pounder, 1985; Prasad & Lloyd, 1983; Salmons, 1984; Sims & O'Brien, 1979).

3

Choosing this method of suicide appears to be determined by saliency; that is, the jump site was accessible and/or suggested through recent publicity. Hendin (1982) suggests that socialization, availability, cultural acceptance, and the personal, symbolic meaning of the act or setting all play an interactive role in an individual's choice of method. Thus, that 50% of all completed suicides among black residents of New York City are by jumping may be explained by the observation that many important aspects of black life in New York City occur in the context of crowded, multistoried tenements. Seiden and Spence (1982), in their analysis of jumping suicides from the Golden Gate Bridge in San Francisco over a 43-year period, conclude that of Dublin's three factors determining suicide method, personal psychological/symbolic factors were more decisive than accessibility and social/behaviorial suggestion (Dublin, 1963). Supporting this conclusion, these authors noted that 58 individuals actually had crossed the Bay Bridge (an equally lethal jump site) in order to get to and jump from the Golden Gate Bridge.

The National Research Council's *Injury In America* (1985) notes that little is known about the prevention of injuries from falls from heights. Also, in spite of the recommendation of the Task Force on Youth Suicide to "limit access to and modify lethal means of suicide" (U.S. Department of Health and Human Services, 1989), restricting access to high places was not deemed by a panel of experts to be a significant intervention to prevent youth suicide (Eddy, Wolpert, & Rosenberg, 1987).

When considered from a perspective broader than that of youth suicide, however, there are some promising preventive measures. Most studies of suicide by jumping suggest that protective barriers may reduce or prevent injury due to falls from elevated structures. Seiden and Spence (1982) specifically state that protective barriers have substantially reduced or eliminated deaths by jumping at several international "suicide landmarks." Pounder (1985) points out that a safety fence at Sydney Harbour Bridge in Australia, installed in 1934, has reduced the incidence of fatal falls to 1% of their previous level. Glatt, Sherwood and Amisson (1986) report on the apparent effectiveness, and for considerably less cost, after one year's use, of two suicide phone lines installed on the Mid-Hudson Bridge in Poughkeepsie, New York. Their preliminary report was quite encouraging: of 14 potential jumping suicides, 4 completed their jumps, but 9 used the phones and subsequently were brought in by the bridge police for psychiatric evaluation and treatment.

The following case poses the problem of prevention of suicide by jumping in the context of modern building construction. Increasingly, architectural design appears to favor the open, internal atrium as a mode of aesthetically pleasing construction. The proliferation of these atriums, particularly noticeable in newer hotels, literally has brought the problem of suicide into quite public view. Concurrent with this visibility has come the demand for consideration of better environmental controls to prevent such suicides.

CASE STUDY: A SUICIDE LANDMARK

The Site

A centrally located, prominent government building housing the county administration and courts in a large metropolitan area. During construction there was considerable and well-publicized controversy over its design. The building is 24 stories high with an open internal atrium extending all the way up to the roof. The atrium is readily accessible from surrounding walkways and connecting bridges.

The Problem

Within 3 years of its completion, there were three suicides and three suicide attempts in the building, all receiving extensive media attention. Government officials are predominantly interested in protecting "innocent bystanders" as well as preventing suicide. The building's security manager feels that efforts at suicide prevention in the building would be futile because "people can get to it elsewhere or by other means if they really want to." Considerations of cost and aesthetics also mitigate against significant alterations to the building.

Proposed Solutions

Several proposals might be considered; however, each has pros and cons:

1. Entirely enclose all levels and bridges with glass. This offers the most protection but is very expensive and would necessitate changes in heating and ventilating systems.
2. Screen in levels and bridges with metal mesh screens: considered less desirable aesthetically and still quite expensive.
3. Install a glass or plastic transparent roof over the public service level. This would protect people on the ground floor but would not prevent jumps. Maintenance and cleanliness would be a problem; "if a suicide did occur the ceiling would be very nauseating."
4. Arrange a permanent roped-in floral exhibit on the ground floor: would not prevent suicides but would protect bystanders.
5. Put a circus-type net over the public service level (or one every three

three floors): relatively cheap but "would not enhance building aesthetics" and might actually encourage jumping.

6. Increase security, with one guard stationed at every level open to the atrium: effectiveness considered only moderate and cost "astronomical."
7. Use closed-circuit TV: considered ineffective even if cameras were positioned at each level.
8. Place an electrified fence at railing and bridges, designed to give prospective jumpers an electric shock.
9. Install seating on all levels and bridges so that more people would be around to notice and prevent a would-be jumper.
10. Install 9-foot-high glass barriers on all levels and bridges: would not be absolutely foolproof but would deter jumpers, who would have to be acrobatic to scale the wall; aesthetically acceptable at half the cost of complete enclosure, but cost would still be approximately half a million dollars.

As a consultant, what recommendations and rationale would you offer to deal with this problem?

COMMENTARY

Benjamin H. Read:

I have a keen personal interest in the subject under discussion. My personal interests are based on the suicide of a much-loved daughter who dropped to her death from a high bridge in Washington, DC 8 years ago. After a long struggle, the District of Columbia government constructed safety fences at that bridge 6 years later—an action still being contested on appeal in court by opponents of the barriers, even though suicides there have been drastically reduced.

The managers of this large Hyatt-like county government building that we are considering may think they have a choice between doing nothing and taking some form of preventive action, but they are mistaken. Politics, the media, law, ethics, common sense, and the virtual certainty that there will be additional suicides or suicide attempts from the walkways and connecting bridges overlooking the atrium will eventually compel them to take reasonable preventive actions.

The standard argument voiced here by those favoring the status quo, that people determined to commit suicide will just go elsewhere to do so, is not persuasive and does not alter my conclusion. In all likelihood some will end their own lives elsewhere, but many will not: some will find that changed circumstances have reinforced their will to live. To allow a publicized suicide site to remain without safeguards at the very seat of local government, where elected or appointed officials reponsible to the electorate conduct public affairs, is not a politically tenable position. I would also observe that this is a building where many residents come or are forced to come to court daily, some of whom undoubtedly are at increased risk for suicide because they have and will suffer serious personal setbacks when denied the judicial outcome or administrative relief they have sought.

The only political factor that would change my prediction that preventive action must be taken would be that the view form any of the open lookout points over the atrium commanded a unique and breathtaking view particularly favored by the public or that the balconies and bridges were so distinctive as to be observed with affection from the outside as well as inside the structure. These factors and alleged engineering problems have blocked all efforts to place safety measures at the Golden Gate Bridge despite the horrendous average toll of 24 known suicides per year since its construction in 1937 plus an unknown toll of those whose deaths there are never witnessed. But who ever heard of a government building in our land that had such attributes!

Another factor that could at least delay preventive action is absent in our case. This building was constructed only 3 years ago. It would have to be 50 years old to be eligible for historic preservation status, which could be expected to ensure a fair-sized army of opponents of any design change. But that is not a consideration in our case.

In my opinion the only real issue for debate is whether the safety measures to be taken will be reasonably effective.

Only 2 of the 10 proposed solutions listed in the case write-up can meet the cost and aesthetics criteria established and, I would add, the essential test of effectiveness. Those options are complete glass enclosures or 9-foot-high glass barriers on all atrium levels and bridges. A variant of a third listed proposal, for "metal mesh screens," is also worth consideration, as I will note shortly.

I would recommend installation of the 9-foot glass barriers at a cost of $500,000. I do so based on the three cited criteria.

Cost

Although a half-million-dollar outlay may seem horrendous to the county treasurer in a time of shrinking public resources, I would predict with confidence that that sum would look attractive compared to the size of a likely jury damages award in a suit against the local government for willful negligence in a wrongful death or injury action brought by the survivors and dependents of the person who has died from the fall or been killed or injured by a falling body. If I were an active plaintiff's lawyer, I would accept such a case on a contingency fee basis without hesitation if the local government had not taken reasonable and timely preventive actions.

The three prior suicides and three attempts in the short 3-year period in which the building has been open amount to full legal notice to the county that appropriate public safety measures are needed. If the county's lawyers looked into the matter, they would find that in an increasing number of jurisdictions around the country, preventive safeguards have been installed at high, publicly controlled places that have become notorious magnet sites for suicides.

The Empire State Building administrators fenced their 86th floor observation platform after 16 suicides between 1931 and 1947. Authorities at the Seattle Space Needle revolving restaurant and observation platform installed preventive measures after the first two suicides occurred there in 1974. The John F. Kennedy Library in Boston has been equipped with glass barriers on the railings of its nine-floor atrium since its construction 8 years ago. When the Old Post Office Building on Pennsylvania Avenue in Washington, DC, was renovated 4 or 5 years ago, unobtrusive high-tensile aviation wires were strung 6 inches apart, from the ceilings to the railings of the 12-floor observation tower with its open windows, and they have prevented all falls. This is an additional option that should be explored because it may be both less expenive and more effective than partial glass barriers and only slightly less aesthetic.

Public authorities with responsibility for the entire federal highway system now routinely require 9-foot-high fences on bridges and overpasses, and local governments have installed barriers where multiple suicides had occurred at high bridges over the Cape Cod Canal, Pasadena's Colorado Canyon, and Washington's Rock Creek Park at the Duke Ellington Bridge.

The status quo is not a cost-effective option in the long run in the case under review.

Aesthetics

Glass safeguards are plainly the best option from an aesthetic viewpoint for reasons that do not need spelling out. Shatterproof or bulletproof glass panels are available, as are thinner glass panels reinforced by inset high-strength, unobtrusive wiring.

For anyone who has the slightest fear of heights, and I am sure that we have all seen such persons cowering in the rear of those open atrium elevators so prevalent today or walking timidly far back from the edge of high atrium walkways and bridges, the aesthetic impact of glass safety barriers can be a welcome improvement rather than an intrusion on enjoyment.

One of the proposed solutions involves placement of circus-type nets over the floor level of the atrium and at every third floor up to the roof. These would be ugly trash-collectors that would clearly set every aesthetic nerve on edge throughout the metropolitan area and raise a storm of opposition and derision. But it is important to recognize that courts have an obligation to weigh competing public interests. Aesthetic considerations alone have seldom if ever been allowed to override the demonstrated requirements of public safety.

Effectiveness

Experience elsewhere in the United States indicates that barriers of 9 feet or more, without intermediate-level footholds, have been effective in stopping suicides at bridges and overpasses. Barriers that consist of 4- or 5-foot fences or barriers on top of 3- or 4-foot existing railings, which permit foothold, have sharply reduced but not ended suicides at other dangerous high locations.

Even though it might be possible theoretically for a person with acrobatic prowess to scale a 9-foot sheer-glass barrier, it seems unlikely, and the deterrent effect of such barriers would be tremendous.

Suicide by dropping from high places is the one prevalent method of self-inflicted death that requires no advance planning or equipment—no gun, no rope, no pills, or other lethal agents. As such it poses a particular hazard to those suffering from transitory kinds of depression or despair, particularly when exacerbated by drink or drugs.

One thing we've learned since the tragedy that struck our family is that the final act of suicide is most often approached with deep ambivalence. Dr. David H. Rosen, a psychiatrist now at Texas A&M, has interviewed 9 of the 19 persons known to have jumped from the Golden Gate Bridge and survived the fall. All recounted the doubts that tormented them until the moment they fell free, as well as the instant and deep regret they experienced. The sustained efforts required by most persons to scale a high barrier require a concentrated determination for self-destruction that would not withstand any ambiguity of intent. And in some cases the time and difficulty involved in scaling the barriers would provide opportunity for rescue.

Many of the other proposed solutions fail the test of effectiveness.

- Transparent covers over the ground floor of the atrium would probably not protect those below from a body falling from even the second floor, much less from higher-velocity falls from up to the 24th floor.
- Roped-off sections of the ground floor might afford some protection for passersby below, except for those in the entry ways to the atrium;

but, of course, both this and the prior option are seriously deficient in not even attempting to prevent suicides.

- Round-the-clock guards at every level open to the atrium would be astronomically expensive, and it is a delusion to think that such guards would be on constant alert; even if they were, they would rarely be at the exact spot needed to prevent a suicide. In fact, ill-timed, sudden intervention can precipitate suicidal action, as happened in the case of my daughter when a well-intentioned police officer reached out to stop her.
- Closed-circuit TV monitors would be less effective than guards on every floor because any possible help would be more distant.
- Seats near the open spaces to increase the likelihood of random intervention by citizen samaritans who might be relaxing there would be still less effective.
- And finally, electric shock railings would guarantee a legion of complaints and other complications even if they worked as intended.

For all of these reasons, I would conclude that the most feasible and appropriate solution is the construction of the proposed 9-foot glass public safety barriers.

Richard Seiden:

With respect to developing an effective suicide prevention program in public places, two basic questions must be considered: (1) Why do certain sites acquire reputations as suicide magnets (for example, many communities have hanging trees or lover's leaps; in San Francisco, we have the Golden Gate Bridge); and (2) will preventing suicides at that particular spot simply shift the suicides to another site? (The familiar "They'll just go someplace else" argument is expressed by the security manager of the building cited in our exemplary illustration.) Let us begin with a brief and selective review of the historical experience with suicide landmarks and their control.

The Empire State Building in New York City was the location for an outbreak of suicides in which 16 persons killed themselves by jumping from the tower during the years 1931 to 1947. Most of these cases occurred during the post-World War II period (1945–1947) and resulted in the construction of an observation tower fence that curves in at the top. Since this fence was constructed, it has greatly reduced the number of suicides from the tower. Accurate statistics are difficult to come by because of the extremely wary position of building management, but there do not seem to have been more than two suicides since construction of the fence and the later addition of a security guard.

A large general medical hospital is cited by Litman and Farberow (1970) as the site of 25 suicides in the 6-year period from 1955 to 1961. The unnamed hospital located in a large U.S. city, called on the Los Angeles Suicide Prevention Center for advice in January 1961. Because 23 of the 25 hospital suicides had occurred by jumping from windows, the consultants recommended that mechanical "stops" be installed in all windows. In the remainder of 1961 there were only two suicides, and both patients had to smash a window to jump to their deaths. In the ensuing years there were no reported suicides, according to the authors.

The Arroyo Seco Bridge, as its name suggests, is an overland span bridging a water-carved gulley near the Pasadena Rose Bowl. From 1913 to 1936, 80 people jumped to their deaths from this bridge. After considerable public and journalistic criticism, the bridge authorities constructed a hardware fence barrier, and to my knowledge there has been only one further suicide from this location.

The Berkeley Campanile, symbol of the Univeristy of California campus, was the site of two suicides within a matter of days. When a campus gallows humorist painted a bull's-eye at the base of the tower, the point was made, and the tower was closed to the public until a Plexiglass barrier was installed. There have been no further suicides.

Mt. Mihara on the volcanic Japanese island of Oshima holds the dubious record for self-destructive landmarks. Presumably more than a thousand persons killed themselves by jumping into the crater and dying of the poisonous fumes, all of this carnage telescoped into a brief 3-year period, 1933–1936. The epidemic was quashed when the government placed barbed wire around the edge of the crater and reinforced the prohibition with armed guards in machine gun nests to control the situation!

In each of these situations it was noted that doing nothing, looking the other way, wishing the problem away, just did not work. When the situation remained unmodified, the location began to develop a macabre reputation, acting like a magnet to the emotionally distressed and suicide-susceptible, drawing them to their self-inflicted deaths. Yet in every case in which physical barriers were installed, the epidemic subsided. In the cases of the Campanile and Mt. Mihara, the physical barriers were removed after a period of time, and no new wave of suicides occurred; so timing is apparently a very critical factor in dealing with this problem. The exact reasons that some places develop a fatal reputation are not abundantly clear, but there is some concern that publicity of a sensational sort may be a component in this complex equation. Perhaps it is a fact that people may achieve a kind of notoriety and attention in death that they did not receive in a lifetime of despair and depression. Research on the effects of publicity has been a mixed bag. However, in the Bay area, the newspapers have taken it upon themselves not to feature the running box score of jumpers from the Golden Gate and Bay Bridges in a flamboyant manner.

What about the appealing common sense argument that they'll just go someplace else? This untested assumption does not hold up under the weight of clinical or research scrutiny. We know full well that suicidality is not an inexorable process; suicidal people are highly ambivalent: they want to live, to die, to perish, and to be saved; there is a fight between the forces of life and death rather then an unwavering desire to self-destruct. Moreover, the danger period is acute and transitory rather than chronic and pervasive. To document this we have only to look at what happens to those rescued or otherwise prevented from completing their suicide. The classic studies by Stengel (1968) and by Ringel show a low proportion of attempters (5–10%) who eventually complete their suicides after follow-up periods of 15 to 20 years (Stengel, 1968). My own research on persons restrained from jumping off the Golden Gate Bridge indicated that only about 4% went on to kill themselves after a follow-up period of more than 20 years. To phrase it more optimistically, 96% of this high-risk group of attempters found the strength to muck it through without killing themselves. Probably the most convincing argument for the environmental modification approach[1], or the "technological fix," as its detractors call it, comes from the amazing experience in the British Isles. For years, the favored method of suicide in England and Wales was to kill oneself by putting one's head in the oven and turning on the lethal coke gas, rich in deadly carbon monoxide. Each home was equipped with its own convenient little execution chamber equivalent to the loaded gun you don't want to have around the house in times of depression. In the early 1960s a serendipitous event happened: England discovered vast fields of petroleum and natural gas in the North Sea. The discovery was to have profound effects, not only on the British economy but on the suicide rate as well. The English shortly thereafter began converting their domestic gas stock from the deadly coke gas to the relatively benign natural gas, and the suicide rate began dropping proportionately. By the time the switchover had been accomplished, the suicide rate had dropped a remarkable 33% below its former level and, even more important, it has stayed there despite the opportunity for the suicidally bent to change to other more effective methods. All of this has occurred against a background of rising rates worldwide and a domestic picture character-ized by unemployment, social tensions, and other variables that should have propelled the suicide rate upward. To my mind, the lesson to be drawn is that much of suicidal behavior is adventitious once a threshold

---

[1]In contrast to changing "the hearts and minds" of people, we are changing the outside environment, analogous to seatbelts, which do not make a better driver but do save lives in the event of an accident.

level has been reached. And when a lethal means of suicide is available, it will be used in momentary fits of depression or impulsivity. (An exact analogy can be made here to the related phenomenon of homicide, which is directly connected to the number of household firearms in circulation. The more guns, the more homicide deaths.)

Finally, it should be appreciated that suicide attempters, especially those drawn to landmark locations, have a particular and highly personal plan, usually one involving a strongly and personally symbolic site. Our Golden Gate Bridge attempters had carried this particular fantasy around in their heads for long periods, and when asked what they would have done if their fantasized method was unavailable, they invariably responded that they would have had to rethink their plans. They did not propose to change gears capriciously and jump off some other place. No, they would have to disband their plans at least for the short run because another location did not fit the repetitively fantasized demise they had nurtured for such a long time.

Our review of previous experience leads us to the following conclusions: (a) certain locations, if unmodified, can act as fatal magnets that draw the suicide-prone; (b) physical barriers will drastically reduce the suicide deaths at these locations; (c) barriers may not need to be permanently emplaced; (d) there is ample evidence that the ambivalence and acuteness of suicidal behavior lead to a favorable prognosis for persons apprehended or rescued from suicide; (e) there is little if any evidence that they will inexorably go elsewhere to complete the deed; and (f) suicidal fantasies concerning particular locales seem highly specific and tied to that site; they seem to have a deep personal signficance and therefore, are not easily transferred.

Accordingly, I would make the following recommendations with regard to the public building in question:

1. Because our first concern is and ought to be the protection of innocent passersby, I would concur with Proposal 4, to establish a permanent roped-in floral exhibit on the ground floor to protect bystanders. This has the virtue of being effective as well as aesthetically pleasing.
2. I would work with the media to reduce the "extensive media attention" that the building was receiving.
3. I would stress that it is important that something visible and significant be done at once. The increased security discussed in Proposal 6 would present that highly visible indication that the problem was recognized and steps were being taken to control it. Although the costs might be "astronomical," it might not be necessary to continue this increased security for more than 2 or 3 months.
4. My choice for the long term is Proposal 10. The 9-foot-high glass

barriers would be cost-effective, aesthetically acceptable and enough of a deterrent to discourage all but the most determined jumper.

5. Finally, I would point out, as did Mr. Read, that such steps, although perhaps regrettable, are necessary, not only from a humanistic point of view but also as a defense against the legal actions that could very well arise if nothing were done to prevent further suicides.

James Moyer:

My background is in the business community, having safety and security responsibilities for a company that has a lot of atriums in its hotels. Marriott has about 345 hotels, 25 of which have atriums. In addition, we have about 140,000 rooms that are above ground level and have balconies. If individuals wanted to commit suicide by walking out onto their own private balconies and jumping, they could.

So what is the record? In 1987, within Marriott, we had 11 suicides; in 1986, we had 4. The number of suicides in our company appears to have increased. These are not the numbers of those jumping, however. We have had one suicide by jumping in 1988. I was directly involved with managing that, not on the scene, but in resolving the issues associated with subsequent prevention and management.

My experience tells me that the act of suicide is a "private" action attempted by people who believe that this action is the answer to a situation they are forced to resolve; the act of "public suicide" often is an action pursued by individuals who wish to undertake this solution and to draw attention to themselves. It also is an impulsive act and is very difficult to control in a building that has public access, where people can and must enter in a free and open manner. Clearly, people think about jumping from a building because they have read, seen, or heard about this specific method of suicide. In talking with some surviving family members and investigating officers, in almost every case I can recollect, those who have jumped have done so as a result of previous knowledge of the incident occurring at that facility.

Background Information

There are really six key points that I, as a security professional, would ask myself or ask the person working on this particular property to find out:

1. What steps were taken to stop the three attempted suicides?
2. Are there common factors of these successful preventive efforts that can be further explored to improve the security of the atrium area?

3. Likewise, what common characteristics exist in three successful suicide attempts?
4. What can be learned from these incidents?
5. Perhaps most important, why did the suicides and the attempts attract media attention?
6. What has been done to ensure that no media coverage beyond a small "Page 10, Section G" article in the back of the local newspaper is actually published?

If I were to have this happen in one of the facilities that Marriott is responsible for, we would meet with the people involved and ensure that the objective of the investigation would be to minimize the risk of attempted suicides on the property in the most cost-effective manner possible.

There are a number of control measures I would recommend implementing before considering the alternatives described in this case scenario.

The Peachtree Plaza Hotel—a great big glass cylindrical building that began the birth of the downtown convention business in Atlanta—was the scene of several suicides and attempts in the first years of its operation. It was the landmark facility. This hotel management got their problem effectively under control in these ways:

First of all, and most important, they implemented an agreement with the media and authorities in the city to stop making suicide an attractive event and not to cover it as front page news. They did all they could to stop all public review of such incidents, including editorial columns and interviews with building and security professionals.

Second, they implemented suicide prevention efforts that surfaced from factual analyses of the successful and unsuccessful attempts. For example, the following control measures could be implemented in the case under discussion:

1. Increase patrols at critical times. We might have found from our research of three suicide attempts and three completions that there was a key, critical time when these events occurred.
2. Specifically, patrol floors above floor 10, as an example.
3. Prohibit building entry by means other than the core elevator bank.
4. Identify suspects by behavior or appearance, and follow up. This is a common control method that we use in our hotels, and I think we do this very successfully. One way is to station a permanent security post at the elevator landing at lobby level and train the security officer on "eye contact" and "verbal intervention" controls. In some hotels a "question every 10th person" control method is used. If you happen to be the 10th person when you visit one of these hotels, you are going to get a very friendly conversation. The answer to the question "May I help you

please?" or "Can you tell me which particular location you'd like to go to in our building?" will quickly get you to the right place if you have business in the building and quickly get you into a confrontation with a security professional if you don't answer the question right. The point is that these control measures can be implemented without a great deal of additional expense in a hotel or anywhere else, and they tend to make that facility less attractive as an opportunity for people to commit suicide.

5. Increase professional law enforcement presence by moving the closest police substation office quarters into the building on floor 1 of this modern new government building. Their appearance and their presence, would deter suicidal individuals from going into that building.

6. Finally, I would slightly modify the building if I could not get it under control. My view would be to adopt Point 4, "An exhibit in the lobby." From a risk-management, public safety, and liability-control (i.e., wrongful death) point of view, the city's obligation is to the building occupants, that is, those who would be injured by people who jumped. I would get them out of the way and install a rock garden in the lobby. Beyond that I would also erect barriers that prevent people from taking the opportunities to jump. In our facilities we do not erect 9-foot barriers. In many of our facilities we build what are called—please excuse the expression—"cattle catchers." These are angular devices that you actually have to crawl out on in order to jump. Do they prevent someone from actually doing that? No, but they do two things: As they are filled with planters, a potential jumper first is going to knock planters down, and second, he or she is going to take time. Time is the antithesis of impulsivity.

The final question is, from a business management standpoint, is it the responsibility of business and government to prevent suicide by jumping from hotels or government buildings with atrium lobbies? I don't know whether that question can be answered until you ask the more fundamental question, which is; is it the responsibility of a private organization (or private entity) to protect the public welfare? The answer to that question has got to be yes! So what we have to see in private-industry buildings with beautifully designed atriums is some middle ground: we erect structures and implement control measures that minimize risk. The bottom line: You will never prevent all suicidal behavior; you must seek to move forward to reduce the frequency of such events.

Questions and Responses

Q: I am somewhat ambivalent about the total-prevention approach. I have been committed to the prevention of suicide all of my professional life and to bringing troubled people into the mental health system who otherwise might be unknown to it (until the time they become a statistic, i.e., a suicide). My concern is with eliminating a potential site in order to bring people into care. In the building we are discussing in this case, I wonder whether we can use the reputation of this as a suicide site to bring troubled individuals into the mental health system to get the care they need.

By analogy, in our experience in Poughkeepsie, New York, which has a bridge structurally very similar to the Golden Gate and from which about three to five people have committed suicide annually since its opening, it was impossible architecturally to install barriers of any kind except at exorbitant cost. Instead, for about $5,000 we installed a two-way radio device connecting the bridge with our psychiatric emergency service, which is operated 24 hours a day by trained psychiatric staff. What we have found over the past 3 years is that the suicide rate has, in fact, gone down. Rarely a month goes by without somebody using the phone; and in the 3 years, 44 people have been brought in to our service for psychiatric care, 22 of whom were immediately hospitalized. They had been unknown to the system and were in need of immediate psychiatric care.

So the question I raise is this: If you were totally successful in preventing suicides at this particular site, would not the ambivalence that Dr. Seiden talks about—the self-wrestling, the desire to eliminate one's life, the belief that help is impossible in spite of the desire to be rescued and the desire to reach out for help—be transferred someplace else? Ultimately, the people who might have attempted suicide at that site would move on only to commit suicide someplace else at another time. I wonder if, in fact, the circus net, spaced at several different floors, is not the best solution. People are not going to jump off the side with a circus net in place unless they are truly troubled, in need of bringing their case to the attention of the authorities, and, in fact, can be rescued. It is a face-saving way to bring one's distress to the attention of public officials and is ultimately a nonlethal call for help. Thus, we not only have prevented a sucide, but we have gained what is possibly a therapeutic contract.

A (Seiden): That is an interesting argument: that the site acts as a catchment area and therefore can centralize and focus potentially troubled people. That "they will only go elsewhere" was used as an argument for doing nothing, of course, with the Golden Gate Bridge. Your response of hospitalizing such people and giving full weight to their problems is quite different from what typically happens. For example, at the Golden Gate Bridge they are simply rounded up and sometimes released to relatives, to friends, or just to themselves. Sometimes they are taken to the nearest mental health or catchment facility and then released, only to come back maybe an hour to two later. So it actually depends on how much follow-through there is. I know that in our case nothing happens once they're apprehended, so it isn't really a salient argument. In your case it may be. But I still don't like the idea of a net. I have a feeling it would attract a lot of college kids who would try to jump into it on weekends.

A (Read): The one place that a net has been tried, that I know of, is the Seattle Space Needle, after they had two suicides in 1974. They put up a fisherman's net in an outreach position. There were cries of protest that it looked like a wharf up on high and that it was catching all kinds of things: leaves, debris, and God knows what. They had to beat a fairly hasty retreat from it, so it obviously depends on the site. When we looked at that alternative for the high bridges over Rock Creek Park in Washington, we immediately had visions of a pregnant cow, that it would accumulate debris and the like and be a horrendous maintenance problem. It might be less of a maintenance issue in an interior structure, but I think that there would be real aesthetic problems for those looking from the atrium.

A (Moyer): I believe that the appearance of the net could be aesthetically handled without much problem; but where nature would contaminate the nets outdoors, our customers would do so indoors (especially on college weekends students would throw stuff down from their rooms). From an operational standpoint, it would be very effective in a building. My comments today have been focused on my own industry; in a public building it might be a bit more of a controlled environment than it would be in a facility like a hotel.

Q: Thinking of this problem from a very basic primary prevention standpoint, are any of the panelists aware of any efforts to sensitize schools of architecture to the importance of combining aesthetics with suicide prevention?

A (Seiden): I am not aware of any school involvement; but, for example, with the proposed suicide barrier for the Golden Gate Bridge, we did have a design contest. It was sent out to various architectural firms, and plans were requested. There was an actual competition, and a design was chosen. It proposed thin stainless steel rods held under tension and canted at a certain angle so that you had an unimpeded view of the bay as you were driving by, which caused one of the bridge directors to say that this would increase traffic accidents on the bridge. There is an argument for everything. It was really a matter of bad faith because the bridge authorities eventually rejected the design. They did build the mock-up of this design, and it is down in a ravine someplace, out of sight. They brought in mountain climbers, believe it or not, to see if they could scale this 8-foot-high barrier. Of course, they could, but a healthy mountain climber is not the same as a person who is in the midst of a depression.

Then they said, "Well, what if someone came on the bridge with a ladder?" I assured them they wouldn't get too far past the toll gates with a ladder. But this is the kind of bad faith and irrationality we have to deal with.

A (Read): I think your idea is an excellent one, quite frankly.

Q: Do you think that building codes ought to be revised? The problem to which we are responding involves repairing or amending a structure that is already built. One might argue that we ought to interfere earlier and amend our building codes to prohibit the construction of such a structure. Do you think that ought to be done, and if so, what degree of constriction (assuming that it would affect Hyatt as well as Marriott) would be required, and would that be a sensible thing to do?

A (Read): The only precedent I can cite is the federal highway system (to which I alluded earlier). The code guidelines there prescribe 9-foot barriers on overpasses and walkways over the highway. The requirements are usually met by the 9-foot mesh fences or complete mesh fence enclosures when the overpass is anywhere near a school or playground, so there is a gradation of those requirements. These barriers are in widespread use throughout the federal highway system and provide good examples of the preventive actions that have been taken from the time of construction.

I do believe—and there perhaps is a slight bit of disagreement on the panel—that there is a a somewhat higher obligation on the part of public authorities who control public space.

Q: What are the obligations of and the possibilities for the American Association of Suicidology (AAS) to urge modifications of building codes or to influence the design of buildings?

A (Moyer): I don't know either the charter or the objectives of the AAS, frankly, but I would suggest that if that is the objective, you would certainly want to try to be involved in the front end of the building design. I would recommend to you that the building codes most closely related to the ones that you are after are the NFPA Life Safety 101 Code, which is a code designed to deal with the issue of life safety primarily as it related to fire emergency safety but also talks about a number of other key aspects of safety in the public environment; and the Universal Building Code, which everyone has to comply with in order to get an occupancy permit to open a building. Both of those codes speak a great deal to public safety. I can't quote the individual section, but I know there are sections associated with public space, protections with regard to space in between vertical ballards, and space between pickets on railings, and so on. That would be a very interesting approach, one in which you could make your contribution, one that I think would be appropriate because this code has been adopted and used universally by the insurance industry to provide adequate insurance levels when people build buildings. That angle makes sense to me.

Comment: Before even getting into the code issue, I think there are two basic questions that have to be asked: (1) whom will the building serve and (2) what can we do to raise consciousness about our concerns? It is one thing to talk about a hotel that serves the general population and another to serve those people in the court system, many of whom are distressed at the time they go into the courts. What this organization can do best is raise the consciousness of people involved in the construction of certain kinds of buildings. In New York State the architects built one of the new state hospitals, the Capital Psychiatric Center in Albany, with an atrium, without any consideration for the fact that this was a building housing psychotic, suicidal, and troubled individuals. It was discovered that the architects weren't taking this into consideration when patients came out of their units and jumped over the side. It was at that point that they put up a netlike structure with a certain amount of pillow-like bounce to it.

Q: Mr. Moyer, in your experience, what do you think has been the most effective and simultaneously most acceptable method that people who build atriums in hotels have found to prevent suicide?

A (Moyer): Without question, the most effective method is to stop telling people about these occurrences, stop putting them in the newspaper. The first thing I do when I get involved in one of these things is that I get our hotel's public relations department to immediately contact the local media and say, "Look, we have an obligation here. What we need to do is quit publicizing this stuff." (My comments here have to do with suicides of all types in hotels because quite often people go into hotels to commit suicide within the guest rooms.) That is the first step. Second, I think architectural modifications that are aesthetically pleasing and are put into the building at the time of construction are the most effective alternative controls.

A (Read): Let me take issue a little bit with Mr. Moyer. I think it is probably worth trying to downplay media sensationalism, but I think it is usually a forlorn objective. I worked for three presidents and four secretaries of state who were often anxious not to have media attention on one thing or another. It is usually a losing cause. All you need is one celebrated human being in distress who takes his or her own life by jumping and it becomes a vain hope to minimize media hype.

Comment: I think I would like to stress what Mr. Moyer said. Because of the success of seatbelts and barriers on freeways and because it will absolutely stop the problem, I think our first reaction to these things is to consider the construction of a barrier. I don't think we need only do what we know is most effective; we can also do other things that affect the hearts and minds of people, including making an effort at least—that is not always in vain—to get the media to cooperate.

Q: A couple of you gave examples of a resulting decline in suicide in areas where barriers have been erected. Do you have any figures on the resulting suicides at similar structures in the general area that we could use when people bring up the contention that suicides will shift to another area? I'm thinking of the Washington experience in particular, high rates at other bridges or in New York City, at other high buildings.

A (Seiden): I 'o, I haven't seen any evidence that they have gone up. For example, after the Empire . tate Building erected barriers, the Chrysler Building and the Rockefeller Center did not have an increase in suicides. Suicides may be so disseminated throughout the area that it would be hard to tell, but I don't know of a case where one kind of landmark has been replaced by another.

A (Read): With regard to the Duke Ellington Bridge in Washington, it has been more than 2 years now since the barriers were completed. There have been three persons, one who climbed around the end of the fence and two who scaled it, but only 1 actual suicide since then. In the equivalent period before the barriers went up, there were 13 suicides. It is too short a time frame, however, with too small a data base, to have confidence that this reduced suicide ratio will continue, but it is certainly a hopeful indication. It might be added that suicides increased in the city in 1986 and were 50% above the national average rate of suicide. There has been no marked proportionate increase in suicides by jumping from other high locations since the Ellington Bridge was fenced.

Comment: In Dutchess County, New York, though we have minimized the number of people using the Mid-Hudson Bridge for suicide, and it has become a place for people to reach out, the suidice rate in the county has remained stable for over 5 years.

A (Moyer): Like anything else that would be of importance to focus the attention of business on an issue, the AAS could begin to collect and maintain statistics on the number of suicides that have occurred in this manner. I understand that this is not being done now. If some organization did collect this data from law enforcement, then, in my opinion, the focus of attention of business would begin to shift to this issues.

Q: Has anybody got any innovative ideas other than phones? I come from a town near Niagara Falls. Phones have been tried at strategic spots. The press does not cooperate. For example, I had a reporter's assurance that if I agreed to be interviewed on television, they would not show somebody who was in the process of taking his own life. Subsequently, they let me down. Any innovative ideas as to barriers or how you can respond to the press?

A (from audience): I suppose that not everyone is familiar with this, but the AAS has a public information committee that has in the last year developed guidelines to be distributed to the press. It comes complete with a press packet. It attempts to educate the press in how to minimize the impact of a suicide without squelching the report. It gives quite specific instructions; for instance; don't print a photograph, don't put it on the front page, do tell where somebody can get help, don't romanticize the details, and so on. So there has been an effort. I don't think it has been successful with the more salacious papers; but it has been with the responsible ones.

A (from audience): Maybe primary prevention is more of an academic issue rather than a reality. What we are really talking about is effective intervention, reaching out to the high-risk person, the would-be suicide, the distraught, at a point prior to that person's vulnerability level being exceeded. Anything that can put troubled people into contact with those who can help is something we should pursue, knowing full well that we're not going to prevent all suicides. What we need to focus on is effective interventions that will bring troubled people into a system that offers them the kind of help they need. From what I know about the phone system in place at Niagara Falls, I think it is doing that; perhaps it's not 100% effective, but there are people who are using it and coming into contact with community mental health centers, at least on the American side.

Q: Unfortunately, on the Canadian side our results are completely different.

A (Moyer): Let me tell you how we get the cooperation of the media because it is no big secret and it might be of interest to you. We don't wait till that event happens and then go to the media. We get them together ahead of time and say, "This is the objective here. From a business management standpoint, we need to minimize news coverage of people jumping out of a Marriott hotel. From a public service standpoint, putting it in the paper with this kind of inflammatory information encourages people to come and look at the place. Maybe some come to commit suicide who had not thought of it before." We employ a public relations firm that has worked closely with the papers, and we also use political influence. We fail some of the time, but more often than not we are successful.

A (Seiden): I'd like to comment on the behavorial clues and cues that have been suggested. I think we can be helpful in developing a kind of suicide profile. For example, on the Golden Gate Bridge we worked with the toll takers and the bridge personnel. Among other things, we use television on the towers. The toll takers are trained to spot the person who is alone, in one place for a long time looking down at the water, and particularly the one who is not dressed for the occasion—scantily clad, for example (it gets very brisk out there). We know such people are oblivious to what is going on in the external environment. Then the bridge personnel will apprehend them, not precipitously but rather cleverly. Instead of using a police car, they go out with an automotive repair truck, as if they are going to get a disabled vehicle off the bridge. Usually, the person will come over to find out what has happened—was there an accident or something? At that point they will restrain them. I think we can be helpful in developing the kind of pattern to look for and how to respond.

A: Our experience on the Mid-Hudson Bridge is identical. With raised consciousness, the New York State bridge personnel have identified people and, in fact, have brought into our psychiatric emergency service six people who did not use the phone at all, but they looked troubled. In each instance these people were hospitalized psychiatrically because they were either psychotically depressed, suicidal, or just psychotic. We can do something to train bridge personnel to identify the high-risk people, to intervene more effectively.

A (Read): I'll mention one technique used by a close relative of mine in Washington, DC. He saw a person looking despondently over the rail of the Connecticut Avenue Bridge. After he had crossed the bridge, he thought, "Oh, my God" and went back. He parked alongside the person, got out of the car, and said, "hey, would you lend me a hand? My battery has gone dead again." Of course, the last thing in the world that the person who is thinking of suicide wants to do is help somebody else, and yet the instinct to do so was strong and he did lend a hand. The ruse worked like a charm. While the person was helping him, my relative said, "I hope you're not thinking of doing something injurious to yourself," and he replied that he had been, but "I'm OK now." It was a technique that might be used in other circumstances.

Comment: One doesn't even have to be too devious about this. If you ask somebody in trouble if they need help, at that point they often will be so appreciative and thankful, they will accept that help.

Comment: I'd like to comment that what this panel has done is more than just elucidate gambits, guidelines, and technology changes; rather, you have made a very strong appeal for public awareness and, in addition, to get to the policymakers and urge them to make changes that will prevent death from high places.

REFERENCES

Berman, A. L., Litman, R.E., & Diller, J. (1989). *Equivocal death casebook.* Unpublished manuscript, American University, Washington, DC.

Dublin, L. I. (1963). *Suicide: A sociological and statistical study.* New York: Ronald Press.

Eddy, D. M., Wolpert, R. L., & Reosenberg, M. L. (1987). Estimating the effectiveness of interventions to prevent youth suicides. *Medical Care, 25* (Suppl. 12), 57–65.

Glatt, K. M., Sherwood, D.W., & Amisson, T. J. (1986). Telephone helplines at a suicide site. *Hospital and Community Psychiatry. 145,* 4469–472.

Hendin, H. (1982). *Suicide in America.* New York: Norton.

Krueger, D.W., & Hutcherson, R. (1978). Suicide attempts by rock-climbing falls. *Suicide and Life-Threatening Behavior, 8,* 41–45.

Litman, R. E., & Farberow, N.L. (1970). Suicide prevention in hospitals. In E. S. Shneidman, N.L. Farberow, R. E. Litman (Eds)., *The psychology of suicide* (pp. 461–473). New York: Science House.

National Research Council and Institute of Medicine. (1985). *Injury in America: A continuing health problem.* Washington, DC: National Academy Press.

Pounder, D. J. (1985). Suicide by leaping from multistory car parks. *Medicine, Science and the Law, 25,* 179–183.

Prasad, A., & Lloyd, G. G. (1983). Attempted suicide by jumping. *Acta Psychiatrica Scandianvica, 69,* 394–396.

Salmons, P. H. (1984). Suicide in high buildings. *British Journal of Psychiatry, 145,* 469–472.

Seiden, R. H., & Spence, M. (1982). A tale of two bridges: Comparative suicide incidence on the Golden Gate and San Francisco-Oakland Bay Bridges. *Crisis, 3,* 32–40.

Sims, A., & O'Brien, K. (1979). Autokabalesis: An account of mentally ill people who jump from buildings. *Medicine, Science and the Law, 19,* 195–198.

Stengel, E. (1968). Attempted suicides. In H. L. P. Resnik (Ed.), *Suicidal behaviors* (pp. 171–189). Boston: Little, Brown.

U.S. Department of Health and Human Services. (1989). *Report of the Secretary's Task Force on Youth Suicide: Vol. 1. Overview and recommendations.* Washington, DC: U.S. Government Printing Office.

2

Suicide Prevention: Clusters and Contagion

Patrick O'Carroll:

Recent suicide clusters among teenagers and young adults have received national attention, and public concern about this issue is growing. Indeed, the intense coverage of certain suicide clusters by radio, television, and printed media has—at a minimum—interfered with community efforts to control these crises. Researchers and suicide prevention specialists have also turned their attention to suicide clusters in order to understand what causes them to determine whether factors exist that could predict which persons are at highest risk in the context of an evolving cluster of suicides, and to define the best way to respond to suicide clusters.

But why all of the attention to suicide clusters? Actually, suicide clusters do not account for many suicides. National mortality data indicate that clusters of completed suicides occur primarily among adolescents and young adults and that even in this age group such clusters account for no more than 5% of all suicides (Gould, Wallenstein, & Kleinman, 1987). Nor are suicide clusters a particularly new phenomenon; suicide "epidemics" have been noted since ancient times and also have been reported from time to time during recent decades (Bawkin, 1957; Hankoff, 1961; Ward & Fox, 1977). Much of the recent attention to suicide clusters appears to derive from the hypothesis that these clusters are caused in party by "contagion" (Robbins & Conroy, 1983; Davidson & Gould, 1989). The term "contagion" has been used differently by different investigators. In general, contagion refers to the tendency of one or more persons' suicide(s) or suicidal behavior to influence another person to attempt or commit suicide. To the extent that contagion causes suicide, efforts to prevent contagion are of critical importance in responding to suicide clusters.

The hypothesized mechanism of suicide contagion has not been well defined. Grief, especially prolonged or unresolved grief over the death of

25

a loved one, is known to be a risk factor for suicide (Bunch, Barraclough, Nelson, & Sainsbury, 1971); (Hagin, 1986), and there are reports that the risk of suicide may be higher among grieving relatives of suicide victims (Cain & Fast, 1972). Imitation may also be a risk factor for suicide. Ecologic evidence suggests that exposing the general population to suicide through television programs or news reports may increase the risk of suicide for certain susceptible individuals, causing a temporal clustering of suicides around the country following such broadcasts (Gould & Shaffer, 1986; Phillips & Carstensen, 1986). Though this has not been found in all studies (Berman, 1988; Phillips & Paight, 1987) and has been challenged in others (Baron & Reiss, 1985; Kessler & Stipp, 1984), the evidence for imitative suicides is certainly suggestive. In the context of geographically localized as well as temporally localized suicide clusters, however, there appears to be a third ingredient in contagion, in addition to grief and imitation. In some suicide clusters, the tendency to glorify suicide victims and to sensationalize their deaths has frequently fostered a community-wide preoccupation, even a fascination, with suicide. The resulting highly charged emotional atmosphere is believed by many to have contributed to causing suicide.

It is this last hypothesized element of contagion that makes it so crucial that we determine how best to respond to apparent suicide clusters. Although the contagion hypothesis has not yet been formally tested at the individual level, compelling anecdotal evidence from investigated suicide clusters suggests that suicides occurring later in the clusters were influenced by the communities' preoccupation with and glorification of suicides occurring earlier in the clusters. Until we have evidence to the contrary, therefore, steps should be taken to prevent further suicides that may be caused in part by the atmosphere, or contagion, of a suicide cluster.

What is the most appropriate response to suicide clusters? This is the question underlying the following case scenario. Though fictional, the scenario is a composite of several real suicide clusters that have been investigated during the past several years.

CASE STUDY: A SUICIDE CLUSTER

Consider a relatively small community (population approximately 30,000) in which three to five suicides usually occur each year. In most cases the suicide victims are over 40 years of age, but there have been instances in which younger persons, including teenagers, have committed suicide. One Tuesday morning in October of a particular year, a 16-year old male committed suicide with a firearm in front of several other students at his high school gymnasium. The victim had been doing fairly well in school and had no known problems at home. He had a number of friends, who stated that the victim had been acting "a little down" but otherwise seemed all right. He had broken up with his girl friend approximately 1 month before the suicide but was not considered by his friends to be overly upset about it.

The suicide caused a minor crisis in the school, with many students feeling distraught over the tragedy and troubled over why such a student would have committed suicide. One of the students who witnessed the suicide (a 15-year-old female) began seeing a psychiatrist because of persistent nightmares about the incident. The school was closed the next day (Wednesday) but reopened again on Thursday. The principal gave a brief eulogy over the loudspeaker that morning and announced that any student who wished to do so might be excused to attend the funeral on Friday.

Things seemed to be returning to normal until, 2 weeks after the suicide, two students in the same high school— a 17-year-old male and an 18-year-old female—died in a single-car collision. They had driven off the road while travelling at high speed late on Friday night after leaving a local party. There was no sign that the driver had attempted to brake the vehicle. The deaths were ruled accidental; it was assumed the driver had fallen asleep at the wheel. Many students in the high school, however, were convinced that this had been a double suicide. Both of the car crash victims had frequently been in trouble in school, and the male student had recently been arrested on charges of possessing marijuana.

These second and third deaths excited a great deal of media interest, with newspaper and television reporters interviewing anyone who would talk to them. One local newspaper reported that at least 8 and possibly as many as 15 suicide attempts had been treated in local emergency rooms in the 2-week period before this second death. An accompanying editorial said that these known attempts were "only the tip of the iceberg." There were increasing rumors of a suicide pact in the school. In response to persistent media requests, a press conference was held by the county coroner, who announced that autopsies revealed that both of the victims had been legally intoxicated at the time of death, and both had traces of marijuana in their blood. This created even more excitement among community members and the media, and parents began demanding that *something* be done to curb this "suicide epidemic."

As a consultant, what recommendations would you make?

COMMENTARY

David C. Clark:

The vignette we are to consider says something about the population (30,000) in the small community and the average number of suicides per year (three to five) but does not make clear how many young people there are in this community. Are there 300 or 3,000 youngsters enrolled in the high school this year? This kind of statistical information is necessary if we are to make epidemiological sense of the events we are discussing. I will argue that the epidemiological approach should guide our clinical and public health planning for apparent outbreaks or clusters of suicides such as this one.

The Epidemiologist's Perspective and Its Practical Value

The epidemiological approach allows us to consider multiple possibilities instead of leaping to a premature conclusion that the events portrayed represent a contagious outbreak of teen suicide in one small community. Considering situations like the one portrayed in the vignette, the *first possibility* is that the number of suicides reported has been overestimated. This is an extremely commonplace occurrence. Once a suicide that is emotionally difficult to accept has occurred, people in the community may become worried, frightened, or panicked to the point where misunderstanding, rumor, and ignorance combine to distort or exaggerate the count of actual suicides that followed the first. In responding to newspaper reporters doing stories on a teen suicide cluster in their communities and in responding to community professionals orchestrating local responses to clusters, I routinely urge them to review the evidence for the number of suicides being reported. It often happens that on careful consideration, several of the "suicides" are nonfatal attempts or gestures, one or two are better understood as accidental deaths (which is the leading cause of deaths for teenagers in the United States), one or two occurred in a different community or a long time ago, and one is rumored but cannot be substantiated.

A *second possibility* is that several suicides can occur by chance within the same jurisdiction in a relatively short period. By jurisdiction, I mean a school, a school district, a small community, a church parish, a county, an Indian reservation, a military base, or whatever other unit of population is the center of focus. The completed suicide rate for adolescents tripled between 1955 and 1977; teen suicide is no longer the rare event that it once was. Though teen suicides occur at a rate of approximately 10 per 100,000 youngsters per year, the laws of probability show that sometimes two teen suicides will occur in a population of 5,000 or 10,000 youngsters within 1 year's time by chance alone. In a metropolitan area like Chicago, it is statistically possible for four or five teen suicides to occur in the same region within several months by chance alone. If a community has not been aware of the occasional teen suicide occurring within its boundaries over the past 10- or 20-year interval, if a community is not aware that suicide is the second or third leading cause of death for adolescents, or if a community is shocked by the suicide of a youngster thought to be "normal," "popular," or "healthy," there may be a predictable panicked reaction to teen death by suicide and a predictable rush to diagnose an epidemic if other teen suicides follow in close order, even though the numbers do not justify concluding there is an epidemic.

A *third possibility* is that a genuine epidemiologically defined cluster has occurred. The suicidologist is in the best position to recognize this case as true when he or she is familiar with the epidemiological figures on youth suicide rates for the nation and for the particular state or county in question, and when he or she has examined monthly and yearly suicide rates for the same age group in that community over the last 10 or 20 years. My impression is that although statistically valid clusters of youth suicide do occur, they are rarer than most people think, and that only one third or one quarter of the situations defined as "clusters" or "contagious outbreaks" can actually be defended as such. Psychometric methods for testing whether a specific number of deaths in a population of specified size constitute a health clustering event or a chance event have not yet been refined.[2] These statistical tools would provide the suicidologist with a valuable mathematical model for quickly and accurately sizing up a number of suicides in preparation for recommending a community response.

Let us review the facts contained in the vignette we are to consider and compare the facts against the three possibilities I have outlined. One 16-year-old has died by suicide, and two other teens died in a car accident that was judged to be accidental. Should we believe the student rumor that the car accident really represents a double suicide? Although I do not deny the possibility, I also think that suicidologists trying to help assess or respond to a community crisis will undercut their own effectiveness by subscribing to rumors.

What about the 15-year-old girl who began to see a psychiatrist, the large number of suicide attempts treated in local emergency rooms, the rumors of a suicide pact in the school, and the growing parental concern?

---

[2]*Editor's note:* Epidemiological techniques to examine time–space clustering of disease events are discussed and critically examined by Gould, Wallenstein, and Davidson (1989).

1. The 15-year-old girl had witnesses the suicide and was having persistent nightmares; the fact that a witness to a suicide would develop a posttraumatic stress disorder (PTSD) and require professional help should not surprise us in the least.
2. The number of suicide attempts has not yet been reliably documented but should be. Although they do not represent completed suicides and may not even forebode another death by suicide (only 1% to 2% of attempters go on to die by suicide each year), they have to be taken seriously.
3. It is, of course, impossible to develop an informed opinion about whether 8 to 15 suicide attempts represent an unusual number during a 2-week period for the emergency rooms polled unless someone has been systematically saving information about teen suicide attempts for just such a purpose.
4. The parental concern is expected and understandable, given the series of events, the rumors, and the provocative newspaper stories.

Thus, my *initial assessment* is that there has been *one* suicidal and two accidental deaths within the high school. At the moment there is no compelling evidence to link the suicide and the car accident. Because suicide is the second or third leading cause of death (depending on the year), and accidental death is the leading cause of death for young people in the United States, the fact that the deaths were all violent is not remarkable in and of itself. The apparent flurry of suicide attempts by teenagers is a source of concern, however, as are the inflammatory newspaper articles and the growing sense of community panic.

The cool and detached perspective of the epidemiologist may seem odd or inappropriate to many clinicians or crisis workers, but the suicidologist will recognize the value of this perspective in such situations. First, this perspective focuses us on a clear-headed analysis of the facts and helps us to separate simple fact from rumor, exaggeration, or distortion. Second, this perspective optimizes the likelihood that we will be able to know when we are confronted with a true cluster and when we are confronted with a "pseudocluster." Third, this perspective assumes a calm, deliberate, and information-based approach to the crisis that is desirable to project to those seeking information and guidance, to community planning committees, to the media, and ultimately to the parents and youth in the community.

Community Fear and Need for Information

But the residents of the community should not be expected to think or feel in epidemiological terms. The aggregation of youthful deaths in one community in such a short space of time has created the *conviction* that there is a cluster of suicides, and therefore this conviction must be responded to and managed astutely. The level of fear and panic in this community has already been allowed to progress too far, and psychological damage will continue to result if the situation is left unattended.

There are at least four reasons why the community response has unfolded the way it has, and it will be helpful to review them if we are to shape a sound response tailored to this community. The first is that grief is more difficult when the deceased is young. The death of a young person violates our sense of the natural order of life and reminds us of the tenuousness and unpredictability of our own life span. In addition, the death of a young person touches many other young persons, who are less developmentally mature and therefore have fewer coping skills for dealing with something most adults don't handle well: the unanticipated and violent death of a friend. It is a hard experience for many adolescents, though the direction and example provided by adults (especially parents and teachers) are very influential. The difficulty of grieving was made even more difficult if the first suicide was sidestepped or hushed up because of adult embarrassment or ignorance and certainly by the fact that two other deaths (albeit not suicides) followed the first by only 2 weeks.

The second reason for the current crisis is that the first youngster who died, the suicide victim, was a "nice kid" who fit no one's stereotype of a troubled or suicidal youngster. This element of surprise or incongruity greatly magnifies the impact of a suicide, although any suicide—but a youth suicide in particular—is shocking to most laypersons. This incongruity frequently leads to the thought that if a youngster so ordinary and healthy-looking could kill himself, then almost *anyone* could be prey to suicide. The premise that *no one* is immune to suicide, that it could happen to anyone at any time or place, and that one is powerless to anticipate or prevent suicide, is so anxiety-provoking that the thought alone can cause a great deal of community unrest bordering on panic.

The third reason that the community reaction took a pathological turn is the ambiguous circumstances of the two accidental deaths. By "ambiguous" I mean that the boy and girl both died in the same accident, that they had frequently been in trouble at school (so they fit the stereotype of the suicide-prone teen better than the first death), that there was no evidence that the driver attempted to brake the vehicle, and that there was so much time for speculation about drug involvement before it was announced (at a press conference!) that both were legally intoxicated and had been using marijuana. It is only natural and human to try to "explain" a suicide in commonsense terms after the fact; that is simply the way humans react. But the more ambiguous the circumstances surrounding the suicide and the fewer facts available to people for constructing their personal explanation of why the suicide occurred, the more their imaginations fills in the details. The more ambiguous the circumstances, the greater the likelihood that people who knew the deceased will assume some responsibility (i.e., regrets, guilt) for things they did or did not do that (in their imaginations) *might have* contributed to the suicide. This kind of guilt can affect a far wider circle of people than just family and close friends, can remain unconscious or barely conscious, and can fan the flames of people's obsessions and fears about the possibility of more suicides.

The fourth reason for the current crisis is the trauma-inducing aspects of the suicide, in which the 16-year-old shot himself in front of several other students in the high school gym. The students and teachers who witnessed the shooting, those who heard the gunfire, and those who saw or handled the corpse at school (where they were totally unprepared to witness anything of the kind) instantly became high-risk candidates for developing PTSDs in addition to and independently of their grief reactions. The vignette we are considering suggests that at least one student who witnessed the suicide, a girl, developed typical symptoms of a PTSD: persistent nightmares.

The work of Dr. Robert Pynoos at UCLA (Pynoos & Eth, 1985) brings a very valuable orientation to situations such as the one we are considering, an orientation that recognizes the *mixture* of grief and PTSD in youngsters exposed to the combined circumstances of death and violence. Pynoos's program includes an evaluation/treatment team prepared to deal with sudden and violent deaths that occur in the presence of a large number of children and adolescents. In a recent research report (Pynoos et al., 1987), Pynoos described an incident in Los Angeles in which a sniper in an apartment building window overlooking an elementary schoolyard opened fire and kept shooting for several hours until police subdued him. At the time of the incident, two-thirds of the schoolchildren had already left school and gone home, but a third were in the school or on the playground. Some inside the building were on the playground side of the building, so they could see and hear what was happening outside their window. As soon as the gunfire erupted, some children on the playground were killed or injured; others remained pinned down and unable to move from fear of being shot. Teachers in rooms overlooking the playground ordered those in the classroom to lie on the floor. No one entered or left the school building for several hours.

In the days immediately following the sniper attack, Pynoos's clinical team went into the school by invitation to screen and help the children over the ensuing months. The research component of their intervention demonstrated that the children at that school frequently experienced two independent syndromes: grief and PTSD. Children who were acquainted with those who died experienced a classical grief syndrome, regardless of their location on the day of the shooting (i.e., on the playground, in the school, or on their way home). Children who were exposed to gunfire or near those who were shot experienced the symptoms associated with PTSD (e.g., nightmares, anxiety states, physical symptoms of anxiety) paralleling the experience of traumatized combat veterans. Some children experienced one syndrome but not the other, some experienced both, and some experienced neither. But the likelihood that any given child was affected by either of the syndromes could be predicted by knowing whether any of his or her friends had died and the location of the child during the incident.

Returning to the small community vignette, there is a high likelihood that those in the gymnasium at the time of the shooting (e.g., gym teacher, classmates), those who entered the gym immediately after the shooting, and those who witnessed the corpse leaving the school were traumatized by what they saw, heard, or felt. It is essential that their special problems be recognized and treated appropriately. Probably all of the students and faculty will have negative reactions on entering the gymnasium for months to come, but their problems will be qualitatively different from those who develop PTSD.

Strategic Mistakes and Ideal Responses

The developmental unpreparedness of adolescents for any grieving, the sudden and violent quality of the deaths, and the incongruities/ambiguities associated with the deaths may not have been dealt with directly or well from the very beginning. School and community authorities were apparently unprepared for events like these, and in reaction they were as stunned and debilitated as the teenagers were. It is not clear that anyone knew how to take charge in the situation; and as a result, opportunities to help the community grieve and digest what had happened were missed, culminating in a growing panic.

What mistakes were made and how should the situation have been managed under ideal circumstances? First, every school (elementary, high school, and college) should have well-developed and updated contingency plans meant to cover a variety of problematic to catastrophic situations (e.g., suicide or violent deaths in or away from the school, natural deaths, natural disasters). The absence of advance planning guarantees that those in positions of responsibility will be forced to respond to crises off the top of their heads, with no game plan, no sense of key personnel to involve in decision making, and no sense of available resources.

School plans should interface with community disaster plans. Some individual and some multiple deaths affect more than just a school community, so advance planning must take into consideration circumstances in which a multi-school, school district, or community response should be implemented. This means that city government, local mental health agencies and professionals, churches and temples, as well as schools, need to maintain some kind of network that they can activate in times of crisis.

The principal in the vignette apparently had to respond to the evolving crisis without the guidance of a preformulated plan. Periods of crisis are not good times for intuiting solutions by oneself; too much is at stake. Ideally, a school crisis plan would identify a handful of key personnel (the crisis team) who would be summoned to meet, assess the situaiton, and make initial plans with the principal in first hour of any crisis. A small committee of heads is better than one head.

I think it was a mistake for the school to close the day following the suicide at school. The students were left to their own devices at the precise time that they were most upset and overwhelmed by their feelings, and the opportunity for a rumor mill to greatly distort the actual events was inadvertently encouraged. I think it was also a mistake to announce the suicide over the school loudspeaker system on the following day, to eulogize the dead youngster at school, and to implicitly recommend that students skip school on Friday to attend the funeral service, whether or not individual students felt a need to attend the funeral.

The loudspeaker system is impersonal and ought not to be used in crisis situations unless it is necessary for safety considerations. Use of the public address system increases the likelihood that no one will have prepared the school faculty for the announcement beforehand; it increases the likelihood that faculty will be as unprepared for catastropic announcements as are the students and thus minimizes the likelihood that the faculty will be able to help exert a positive influence on student reactions by way of example. It is important to avoid eulogizing or memorializing a student who has died by suicide any differently from the way all other deaths are handled, lest the students perceive that the school administration is condoning or sensationalizing the suicide. For this reason I am opposed to awarding those who die by suicide posthumous tributes (e.g., diplomas, varsity letters). The announcement that students who want to attend the funeral service would be excused from school for the entire day may inadvertently encourage those not strongly affected by the suicide to become more involved, promote free and unsupervised time away from school when it will do the most harm, and deprive school personnel of the opportunity to monitor individual student reaction to the tragedy.

The school crisis team, in accord with preexisting plans, should begin monitoring individual student reactions on the first day and for some time to come, establishing a centralized tracking system to identify students who anyone (homeroom teacher, janitor, music teacher, parent) thinks is having a particularly difficult time. Ideally, a school crisis plan defines the appropriate mental health personnel and an office where students who "need to talk" can leave classes to meet with a professional in an individual or group setting. Ideally, the same plan defines groups of qualified staff persons who quickly meet with and examine the students who have been identified as a source of concern, who systematically screen the rest of the student body, and who revise counseling procedures and resources as the situation develops. There must be a carefully thought through "triage" procedure that sorts out the students who are in suicidal crisis, those experiencing PTSD, those showing excessive disbelief, those showing excessive fright, those showing excessive guilt, and those simply grieving.

Because the aforementioned mistakes were made and because counseling/screening services were not available in the school or community after the first death, the community was ripe for reexperiencing the grief and trauma in an intensified way (culminating in a community panic) when the next two deaths occurred so soon afterward. The media magnified the public's preoccupation with youth suicide in a destructive way, at the same time making it evident that a crisis may have been boiling beneath the community's surface for several weeks (i.e., the series of suicide attempts reported for the 2 weeks between the deaths).

The end result, of course, was the sense of a suicide epidemic in the community and a fear bordering on conviction that more children would die. The parents banded together to demand that somebody do something because they all felt as though no one was formulating a response to the crisis. Ultimately, the sense that no one is in the driver's seat of a car speeding out of control only exaggerates the sense of panic that already exists.

Finally, I would recommend that the school and the community study the plan for containing and responding to a suicide epidemic, recently promulgated by the Centers for Disease Control in Atlanta (CDC, 1988) long before any crisis breaks out. The CDC plan emphasizes the need to convene all of the mental health resources of the community early in an epidemic situation and the need to develop a coordinating committee that is responsible for policy, division of labor, and consensual decisons about action. Clearly, the coordinating committee needs to share information with and educate the community, in the process illustrating that a calm but decisive force is in motion. The committee must ensure that territorial skirmishes between community agencies do not develop, but that all persons and agencies pull together in the same direction. The committee should assign several persons responsibility for media relations—to announce important information, to try to suppress publication of destructive or sensationalistic stories, and to develop a close working relationship with the media representatives.

The importance of media relations became apparent to me in Chicago in 1987, following the simultaneous death of four young persons in Bergenfield, New Jersey. A day or two later two Chicago teenagers died together by carbon monoxide poisoning, a case considered a "copycat" suicide by the local press (subsequent information suggests strongly that it was not). After a week or so of extremely sensationalistic newspaper stories of no educative or public health value whatsoever, the director of the Illinois Department of Mental Health convened the editors of Illinois newspapers and TV and radio news departments for a daylong meeting about suicide and media responsibilities. This was not a press conference, and the media were discouraged from sending a beat reporter to "take the story." The assembly was designed to be a high-impact discussion of the issues and feelings raised by a series of suicides in the community and the most responsible way to handle the dilemma. Several newsmen, for example, talked candidly about their personal discomfort in eliciting and passing onto the national newswire sensationalistic details that had no intrinsic news value whatsoever. Many editors were hard-pressed to explain why suicides ought to be covered any differently from other deaths.

From my perspective, the meeting dramatically changed the tenor of news stories thereafter. One major daily, for instance, announced in an editorial that they had adopted a new policy of never carrying suicide stories on the front page and never printing a picture of the suicide victim with the report of the suicide. Each editor has to decide personally what constitutes responsible policy vis-à-vis suicide, but this deliberation may never occur unless the editor is drawn into a forum for thinking about these issues.

Conclusions

For pedagogical purposes, I have assumed a lot about the community's response to the crisis that was not explicit, and I have been more or less harsh in my criticism of deficiencies and mistakes. I have done this to highlight important attitudes, procedures, and opportunities that one should consider when responding to a potential suicide epidemic in one community. But I think it is generally wrong and unproductive to adopt this kind of critical tone when one is faced with a real-world situation of this magnitude. Suicidologists are already well aware of how little we know about suicide and suicide epidemics, so they should not be surprised when nonexperts exhibit uncertainty or ignorance about responding to suicidal crises. In these situations, it is imperative that the suicidologist demonstrate the constructive, cooperative, noncompetitive attitude that should pervade all community assessment, planning, and response efforts. The suicidologist should understand that "Tower of Babel" confusion is always a potential community response to a suicidal crisis and that such confusion is provoked and encouraged by high-handed authoritarian bossiness; by critical evaluation of the ideas, work, or contribution of less experienced or less knowledgeable others eager to participate and help; and by competitive warring over who knows the most, who has the most clinical skills, and which agency is the most qualified to lead community planning.

John E. Meeks:

In the past few years the suicidal act has come "out of the closet." Rather than being a dark secret, carefully guarded, it is widely discussed and rather openly reported in the media. To some extent the professioinal community has been supportive of this social change, feeling that the destigmatization of suicidal behavior could have productive mental health benefits. It was assumed that people considering suicide would be more likely to admit their distress and present themselves for treatment if the act was not viewed in such a negative light.

On balance, it appears that this has not been the outcome. Although the connection may not be direct, certainly greater openness in regard to suicide has been accompanied by a steadily expanding suicidal death rate among the young.

It might be instructive to consider this issue from a somewhat unusual perspective, a perspective different from that of Dr. Clark, although we end with many of the same recommendations. This perspective begins with the observation that many adolescents think about suicide; that suicidal ideation is rather common in adolescence. These thoughts are common because depression is somewhat endemic to adolescence. This developmental period is fertile ground for suicidal ideation because, in addition to depressive syndromes, many adolescents have varying degrees of other vulnerabilities that they bring to this developmental period. In addition, they are moving away from and are relatively isolated from their families, they have yet to form very stable peer relationships, and they have lots of uncertainties about the future and anxiety about adulthood. They have a taste for high drama. Relative to what they will be in 10 years, they are somewhat impulsive and have some difficulty understanding time frames ("Now is forever!"). When they feel bad, it feels as if it will never end. It is a horrible state that they find unendurable. Under severe or continued stress, bereft of adult support and anxious about the dependability of peer attachments, the adolescent may well view suicide as an effective solution to his or her painful dilemma. Because the suicidal act is viewed as a solution rather than the problem, the adolescent may not present this plan in a direct way as a matter for adult intervention and help.

Still, it is obvious that in spite of the unacceptable frequency of suicidal behavior, the vast majority of young people who consider suicide do *not* carry out the act. Suicide is still very rare among adolescents. It may be productive to consider the question of why adolescents do *not* commit suicide. What are the factors operating within the adolescent or in the environment that are protective of the huge number of adolescents who think of suicide but resist the urge to act on the thought?

Deterrents to Suicide

I don't pretend to have all of the answers to that question, but it seems to me that there are some factors that can be recognized. First of all, many adolescents, even in the darkest of times, maintain a hope that things may improve. Fortunately, they have good psychic receivers. If there is a ray of hope, they pick it up. The beam of hope may come from a generally positive relationship with the family (strained though it may be by the developmental period), or it may be based on one or more strong, positive peer relationships. In some adolescents it may be based simply on a clear perception of personal capabilities. Adolescence itself, with its inherent intensity and energy, tends to drive the adolescent toward the hopeful, even in the face of great trouble. Hope may come from adults or members of the peer group who recognize the adolescent's unstated distress or respond to clues that the unhappy adolescent may drop.

As stated earlier, the suicidal adolescent may not ask for help directly because death is viewed as a solution. Fortunately, however, there is often some degree of ambivalence, and adolescents may drop hints in a "Russian roulette" gamble that someone will guess their intent and will support the part of them that desires to continue living. They also hope that in the process of providing help the helper will provide some solutions to the underlying problems. If even one good friend somehow picks up the messages of discomfort and gives extra support, that often may be enough to get them through the crisis.

The second major deterrent to suicidal behavior is the adolescent's recognition of the devastating impact that the act would have on family and friends. Even in the narrowed perception of the suicidal person, there usually remains some recognition of the hostility expressed by the act. Many suicide notes, for example, ask for forgiveness and also offer absolution to those who might feel guilty and view the suicide as a reflection on their care for the young person. Of course, in this sparing of others there is an implied recognition that the suicidal youngster plays a meaningful role in the lives of other people in spite of a sense of isolation. Many profoundly depressed people state that they would commit suicide except that they know what it would do to important others in their lives.

The final protection against suicidal behavior that seems important in many adolescents is the existence of a profound and almost organismic revulsion against the act—a genuine taboo against suicidal behavior. The taboo is experienced as a strong sense that suicide is an unthinkable act; it is wrong, it is strange, it is something not allowable. This taboo has been part of Western society for much of its history and has roots in religion as well as in conventional social expectations.

I have already mentioned that in recent years this taboo has been weakened so that there has been a normalization of suicidal behavior. This single factor may be one of the most important elements that account for clusters of suicidal behavior. It has been recognized that whenever an admired cultural figure suicides there tends to be an increase in adolescent suicide. The adolescent may think, "If it's OK for that person to do it, then maybe it's not so bad. The occurrence of a suicide in the family, particularly the suicide of a parent, has an even stronger impact in legitimizing such behavior as a potential solution to life's pain and problems. In fact, sadly, some efforts to provide preventive intervention, such as showing movies about suicidal adolescents, may have had a negative side effect of making the act more understandable and therefore more acceptable to young viewers who might have been struggling with the suicidal urge.

If there is truth in these observations about deterrence, it would suggest that preventive and interventive efforts should be directed toward discouraging suicidal behavior as an acceptable solution to crisis. The problems that lead to the suicidal frame of mind can be addressed at some leisure if the crisis of suicidality can be survived and the adolescent can live to fight life's battles another day. To be more specific, we are unlikely to eradicate depression in adolescents or eliminate adolescent drug use— or more broadly, the stress and strain of adolescence—all of which we know to be significant contributors to the mind set that can lead to suicidal behavior. However, we can use approaches that would both decrease the likelihood that an adolescent would find suicide an acceptable behavior and illustrate that suicide is a pseudo-, not a real, solution.

These concepts imply a strategy of carefully avoiding glamorizing adolescent suicide. For example, dismissing school for a day or eulogizing the victim would be contraindicated for two reasons: first, because it leaves everybody floating around with a chance to stir the rumor mill, get on the phones and scare each other to death; and second, because what needs to be impressed is that life goes on, and living is what is important. It is living that demands honor and respect, not the voluntary ending of life.

Any kind of memorializing needs to be clearly in a form that would discourage other suicides. For example, if there is going to be a memorial fund, let it be given to suicide prevention or other causes that express clearly the tactful recognition that the youngster's death was sad, regrettable, unfortunate, but by no means heroic. In addition, the recognition of the social unacceptablity of the suicidal behavior may be best augmented by the testimony of survivors. Survivor groups are usually available and more than willing to come forward in the crisis that follows a suicide to convey their personal sense of loss and the profound devastation that suicide inflicts on those who are left behind.

Representatives from these groups can also be helpful in assisting the media in maintaining a constructive response to crises of this kind in the community. Efforts to keep secrets from the press or to distort facts are unwise because they activate the press's suspicion and the healthy desire of the fourth estate to get the facts before the public.

Role of the Media

In cases of suicide, the role of the media is a delicate one. To some extent their proper conduct is problematic because they are a reflection of society. They are the institutionalized expression of our urge to know what is happening and to avoid deception and subterfuge. Because we have some difficulty in remaining level-headed about adolescents, it is no wonder that the press may have trouble in the same area. From the point of view of adults, adolescents have always existed in order to be viewed with alarm. We tend to exaggerate the virtues of young people when we are decrying their innocent victimization; or, alternatively, we comdemn their corruption when we are concerned about their challenge to the social status quo. Adolescents remain one of the few minorities who can be picked on and over generalized about without an organzied defensive response. Therefore, it's hardly surprising that the editorial comment in the local newspaper of our case example could get carried away with inflammatory comments about "tips of icebergs" and "epidemics that must be squelched." However, it is our responsibility to try to assist the media in dealing with adolescent suicide in a manner that will be helpful and will not provoke further deaths. This requires both education regarding the potential dangers of excessive publicity and firm reminders that it is the media's job to report fact and only responsible opinions. This dialogue must always be carried out in a spirit of negotiation and of respect for freedom of information, which, with all of its problems, is still a major foundation of a free society.

I am more cordial to the media than most because I grew up in a newspaper family. From that perspective I have learned that there are a couple of things that are obviously true about the media:

1. With all of its faults and sensationalism, it still is the best protection we have against loss of freedom and deception and many of the

things that are more important than occasionally getting embarrassed or misquoted.

2. The media love hyperbole and "tips of icebergs" and "epidemics of death." Why? Because we, the public, love them; in a word, overstatement sells newspapers. Our media are a reflection of our society. We would be wise to resist the urge to throw the first stone.

In dealing with the media, the best approaches are

1. To educate them. Many newspeople have no idea about cluster phenomena and how the media's overreporting has done damage.
2. To continually reeducate them because there is a fair amount of turnover in the reporting business. It is an entry level job for many young people whose ultimate goal is a less stressful job in the communications industry.
3. To hold their feet to the fire. The media have every right to insist on a "free press" as long as they report facts. You can put considerable pressure on them if they report too much opinion or if editorials begin to get inflammatory. There are pressures that you can bring to bear; you can go around the reporter to someone in control if necessary.

Suggestions

In summary, then, what suggestions can we offer our mythical school or other schools in the real world?

1. Develop a planned response to major emotional crises in the school. The suicidal death of a student is perhaps the most common these days, but other unexpected tragic deaths, resulting from accidents or illness, may be equally disruptive to the emotional development of students. There should be a preformulated constructive plan designed to assist everyone to weather the storm.

2. In the plan, stress small group and individual responses geared to the specific needs of a wide range of students. For example, close friends of the victim need more intensive intervention than do youngsters who were not acquainted with the child. Youngsters who were already depressed or in distress may be more vulnerable to the impact of the death than will youngsters whose adjustment has been happier. The vulnerable youngsters need to be identified and helped. The key thing is to take a diagnostic approach. How close was a given student to the victim? How much of a real, overwhelming stress was the event for that student? How much of a support system does each youngster have? How depressed was he or she, before this happened? Were such students

already at risk before their classmate suicided? These questions are best answered through a sort of concentric circle search, beginning with people who knew the youngster best. They can tell you of others who were strongly affected by the death. You ask each person—friend, teacher, family: "Who seems most upset about this? Who are you worried about?" The goal is to discover and treat those in immediate distress. The first and most important intervention is to make sure nobody else suicides, not to try to cure everybody's long-standing, characterological depression.

3. Involve the community of families. Permitting excuses for any student to attend the funeral of a dead classmate is an important negation of parental rights and responsibilities. Families should make the decision regarding which adolescents should attend the funeral of a dead friend, and the school should permit only those to attend who bring an excuse from home. This makes the family, first of all, aware that their child is so moved by this event as to want to go to the funeral, and it therefore draws them in to give whatever support and help might be needed. Also, it permits them to become involved in the whole of the activity. Families often have information other people don't have, even the students affected most directly, information about what is going on at the moment, the friendship networks in the community, and so on. In a similar way, parents of the victim, as well as of the victim's friends, can be very important sources of information in the effort to identify vulnerable students.

4. The school's plan should include a designated leader who maintains close contact with all elements of the effort to pull things back together, and this person should be provided with adequate consultation from a mental health professional with experience and expertise in the area. This leader should be a school member and must have the total support of the school's administration from the top down. There should be no hidden agenda, no ambiguity as to who really has the power. The possibilities for confusion in these situations are so great that there needs to be clarity provided from the highest adminstrative level. The consequences of confusion may be lethal.

Pamela Cantor:

When I hear the question "Is suicide contagious?" the first thought that comes to my mind is the role of the media. Can televised reports or movies about suicide precipitate other suicides?

I believe the answer to that question is yes. Media portrayal of suicide can be a problem. Sensationalizing a death glamorizes a tragedy and romanticizes a mistake. If broadcasters devote a significant portion of the evening news to a suicide, if we dedicate a yearbook, hold a pep rally, or call off school, then we are sending the wrong message. We are giving "star status" to a person whose behavior was not stellar.

We have to ask for responsible actions from those who are in position to influence our kids. A personal example will help clarify this. I had the good fortune of making a movie. *Young People in Crisis*[3], dealing with the subject of teen suicide. I spent many months arguing with the director over how much "pathos and drama" would go into the script. He wanted "true" stories of suicide and attempted suicide because they would "grip" the audience. "Viewers want violence, tears and emotion," he said. "I want information," I responded. "How dull," he said. But I know that if emotions are too raw, if one is overwhelmed, one cannot learn, and I wanted the film to teach. It took us months to reach a compromise. We used no scenes of suicides, only positive interventions where someone made a difference. We had just enough emotional content to help viewers understand the problem. Maybe the director was right; with more drama perhaps we would have sold more copies. Maybe he was wrong; we could have caused a suicide. I refused to take the chance.

Let me give you another real-life example, one that we modified and used in the movie. Bruce, a high school student, shot himself with a handgun he hid in his school desk. He did this in his schoolroom in front of his classmates and teacher. Of course, the media covered the event. They might have used the air time to tell us about the warning signs; for example, Bruce gave away his favorite record collection. Or the reporters could have told parents how to spot depression before it is too late. Bruce had been absent from school and his job in the weeks before his suicide. He had been apathetic about both. The broadcasters could have outlined ways teachers might intervene to help a distressed student. Bruce let his teachers know he was hurting. He didn't hand in his homework for a few weeks, and he said, "I won't be around much longer. You don't have to worry about helping me make up my work." Or the reporters could have provided information about gun safety and how to keep guns out of the hands of teens. Instead, they used the air time to show us the janitor wiping up the boy's blood. What possible lesson could we learn from this?

Recently, there has been a good deal of controversy regarding television dramas on suicide, generated by an article that appeared in the *New England Journal of Medicine* (Gould & Shaffer, 1986). The authors of this article looked at four dramas on teen suicide and collected data from five New York hospitals on the number of young people who attempted suicide following these shows. They also recorded the number of com-

---

[3]A film presentation of the National Committee on Youth Suicide Prevention and the AAS in consultation with Harvard Medical School (1987). For further information regarding this film, write the American Association of Suicidology, 2459 So. Ash, Denver, CO 80222.

pleted suicides in New York in the 2 weeks that followed each of the broadcasts.

The authors claimed that after the dramas aired, the number of suicides increased. This study made us all think about how media affect teen suicide. Unfortunately, it also makes outspoken members of the Moral Majority and the Eagle Forum think about the effects of education on teen suicide. They reasoned that if television was bad, education too must be negative, and they made concerted efforts to remove all suicide prevention programs from schools.

Those who argue against suicide prevention education say, "If you tell kids about suicide they will do it." This is about as logical as saying, "If you tell kids about AIDS they will go out and request a contaminated blood transfusion." Opposition to education is based on the assumption that education is harmful. But it is ignorance, not knowledge, that is harmful.

This journal study was replicated (Berman, 1988; Phillips & Paight, 1987) in a number of other cities across the United States, and the results did *not* confirm the original study. But, unfortunately, the damage had already been done.

There is little question, however, that what children see on television and in the movies influences their behavior. Teens, in trying to find out who they are and who they want to be, identify with heroes and heroines on the TV screen and on the silver screen. If a movie makes the suicidal character appealing and his solution attractive, this may give disturbed youngsters the idea that they too can solve their dilemma through death. The character and the solution should look unattractive. The movie should not sensationalize; it should instruct.

Let us consider the worst possible scenario. A disturbed teen who is considering suicide watches a movie that portrays suicide, and he then kills himself. This is certainly something everyone wants to avoid, and with preventive efforts it probably can be avoided.

We must, however, also consider the positive side. For each teen such as the one described above there may be 10 who would make a half-hearted attempt after the show, which would bring them help that they otherwise could not ask for. The parents of another 50 teens might come to the realization that their child need help. An additional 100 kids might start to talk to their parents, a discussion that would not have taken place if the show had not given them the opportunity to bring up the subject.

Or there could be 150 teens who will talk to a friend because they want *someone* to notice their problems. And there my be another 200 who, because of the show, realize that they can make a difference for one of their friends.

One of the films studied by Gould and Shaffer (1986) took the precaution of also providing extensive preventive programming. The telephone numbers of local hotlines were flashed on the screen during and after the show. At the end of the movie, the actress who played the victim's mother told viewers about books dealing with teenage suicide. After this particular broadcast, *no* suicides were reported in the area studied. A zero rate of suicide among our young people is just the miracle we want from television.

The second thought that comes to mind is the question of contagion in a school or a community. Suicide *can* be contagious unless we take steps to keep one suicide from becoming many.

The copycat phenomenon was implicated in the rash of suicides reported in such diverse locales as Plano, Texas; Omaha, Nebraska; Scarsdale, New York; and Bergenfield, New Jersey, to name a few in the past several years.

Let me use the Bergenfield incident as a point for discussion. If the situation had been better handled, the four teens who asphyxiated themselves in Bergenfield, New Jersey, in the spring of 1987 might be alive today.

Let me explain. There were four kids from Bergenfield who died the year before these four suicides took place. One was hit by a freight train in June, in what was called an alcohol-related incident. His best friend died the same way 3 months later. A third boy was found in August, drowned. In September, the fourth, Joe Major, died in a 200-foot fall off the Palisades while his friend watched. This also was called an alcohol-related incident. No one acknowledged these deaths as suicides.

The boy who watched Joe fall in September was in the car in Bergenfield in March 1987. One of the sisters in the car had dated Joe. If these four kids had been given the opportunity to acknowledge these earlier deaths as suicides, to grieve and deal with the guilt they may have felt, perhaps *they* would have not had to die. Joe's mother said she thought the four asphyxiations were "in tribute" to her son.

The point is, if the community—friends, teachers, parents—had been willing to talk about the first of these eight deaths in a cathartic, constructive fashion, they most likely would have been able to prevent one suicide from becoming eight.

How, specifically, can a school and community avoid contagion? Our case study allows us to discuss how the mishandling of a situation can cause problems and how the proper handling of the same situation can avoid unwanted tragedy.

As a consultant I have the luxury of looking at the past. This usually means a list of "if only's." What would I have done "if only" I could have foreseen the problems? How could I have handled this differently? Here is my list:

Mental Health Program

I would love to have seen a program of positive mental health education in place in the schools in this fictitious town. You may notice that I did not say a program in suicide prevention education, I said a program in "positive mental health."

In the elementary schools this would focus on affective development. Youngsters would be taught to recognize emotions—anger, sadness, joy—and to express them in a way that others can accept.

In junior high we could focus our efforts on the development of self-esteem. We can teach kids how to feel good about themselves. We can talk about how everyone feels self-conscious and help kids to see ways to bolster each other's ego.

In high school we could focus on learning to deal with stress and developing better coping skills. We can teach kids how to give assertive and clear messages to replace rageful and indirect communications that suicidal youths often use. Young people can learn how to substitute constructive behaviors for angry, antisocial ones. In my opinion, this program should be an essential part of the curriculum. Don't you think it is as important as grammar, math, and social studies?

At the same time, parents should receive instruction in handling and expressing their emotions and in developing communications skills. We particularly need to know how to listen without jumping in and how to get information across without lecturing (which is guaranteed to make a kid tune out).

Teachers also need information. They will be in a better position to deal with a crisis if they know crisis intervention and referral procedures, if they learn how to recognize depression and pathology, and if they have developed a plan of action in the event of a tragedy.

A business would never handle things the way we do in education. A friend of mine who owns a car wash told me he is expecting the industry to be accused of wasting water during the anticipated shortage in the summer months. Rather than just sit around hoping his expectations don't materialize, he organized a meeting of all car wash owners in Massachusetts. He felt they would be wise to examine their water usage figures and develop and emergency plan to present to the state officials in case they are scrutinized. Can't we in education do as well as car wash owners?

Realistically, however, I cannot turn back the clock and I am faced with a difficult situation. What would I advise? What mistakes were committed?

First, the principal closed school the day after the suicide. Where did he expect the students to go? Students need a controlled, safe place. By closing school the principal abandoned them to phone calls, hanging out, and idle hours, perfect for promoting rumors.

And then the principal waited two days to make any announcement. Two days is too long. He should have explained immediately, to his teachers and then to his students, as much as he knew. If students are dismissed without any explanation, they are going to make up their own.

Next, the principal did not hold, but should have held, a community meeting for all students and parents on Tuesday night, immediately following the first incident. He should have had mental health professionals there to answer questions. This would have accomplished three things: provided a forum, offered teens a place to go, and given parents support in answering questions they otherwise might not be prepared to handle.

Finally, he should have phoned the teachers on Tuesday night to call an early morning meeting on Wednesday so that the faculty could deal with their emotions and devise a plan for the day.

Second, the principal gave a eulogy over the loudspeaker. There should be no eulogies; there should be no loudspeaker. More importantly, if he had to make a general announcement, he should have sent children to their individual classrooms so that they could discuss their concerns with a supportive adult. Essentially, the principal made an announcement and signed off.

Third, he gave anyone who wanted to do so the option of leaving school to attend the funeral. How many kids do you think chose to stay in school? This amounts to wholesale dismissal and general pandemonium. He should not have suspended classes.

There was no grief program and no place where kids could safely express their emotions. There was no designated place where kids could go throughout the day to consult staff.

There was no crisis team in place. There should have been one person to talk to the media. There should have been a mental health professional in school for about 3 weeks following the first death. A death, whatever the cause, will be traumatic; and students, teachers, and parents will need support.

There was no identification of kids at risk. Close friends of the students who died or kids who are having difficulties at home or in school should be singled out to receive special attention.

What can schools and communities do to help protect themselves in the future? Schools should set policies that include, at a minimum, the following:

1. If a faculty member knows of an adolescent who has attempted suicide, the student's parents should be told.

2. If there is a crisis at home, parents should be asked to inform the school.
3. If a child has threatened life or limb, rules of confidentiality will not apply.
4. If therapy is needed and a parent refuses, the school should report this to social agencies or to the courts as neglect of psychological and physical welfare.

In addition, a wallet-size card could be given to students and parents at the beginning of each school year, listing the names and numbers of community resources.

One final note: Education is the most effective tool we have. I estimate that suicide prevention education could save about 1,000 young lives each year. If we develop a unified curriculum of affective development, self-esteem development, and coping skills, we could further reduce the number of suicides and, I expect, the number of troubled youths.

Our young people need our help *now*. They should not have to watch us put our heads in the sand and hope the problem will go away; it will not disappear by itself. They need us to plan, at least as well as car wash operators, and use some foresight to save their lives. If we do not plan, we may find ourselves doomed to using consultants and hindsight only to help them through the painful and difficult survival of more unnecessary teenage deaths.

Questions and Responses

Q: With all of these wonderful recommendations, I approach my local school in order to put these into effect. The secretary sees me coming and alerts the principal who says, "Quick, bar the doors, bring down the blinds, we don't want anything to do with it." Principal resistance is a real problem and one that frustrates many of us. Realistically, how do we get to the principal? To get to the teachers you have to go through the principal. Many school principals simply don't want to hear it—not even the word *suicide*. None of this information can be put into effect until we can effectively get to these people.

A (Cantor): Generally speaking, it takes a crisis to wake someone up. Even then they prefer to stick their heads in the sand and pretend the problem will go away. When they recognize it won't, they do something, tentatively, with fear and trepidation. It is the forward-thinking principal who is willing to do something ahead of a crisis. My suggestions include two options:

1. You could be direct. For example, I know of one parent who bought a movie, with her own money, and walked up to the principal and

said, "Here is this movie. I want you to watch it and reimburse me my $75." They did, and then they had an in-service following that which was helpful. She just took the bull by the horns. Probably the school board is the best place to start (not the principal) to get community help.

2. You could be indirect. Institute programs in affective development and self-esteem in the elementary school and, in secondary school, programs in coping with stress and dealing with self-destructive behaviors.

A (Meeks): In two schools in which I was involved it was really the parents who basically told the principal to involve me. They provided me the impetus to enter and develop a program.

Q: I am a school administrator. The very negative comments I'm hearing about school administrators are identical to the very negative comments I hear from school people about mental health professionals. There appears to be a major problem in working together on these interventions. In my county, counselors look at confidentiality first and suicide prevention second. I can't get confidential records or information from the mental health professionals for the special education students and regular education students with whom I am dealing. That has posed a major problem for us. We dealt with this by bringing school and mental health people together. We established a countywide task force of mental health professionals and school people to develop a model protocol that we could share with each of the local school districts. We established training sessions so that we could train four-person crisis intervention teams for each school district. We had exceptional cooperation. Prior to establishing our 4 days of training we made a presentation to all of the county superintendents of schools. After the presentation we had work sessions; 21 districts sent teams. We are continuing with the training. We look at this as a profound beginning.

A (Cantor): It is important not to have an adversarial relationship with each other but to recognize that first and foremost we are all trying to save lives. Second, we know that establishing a crisis team and having plans in effect ahead of a crisis has worked.

Schools that experience the greatest problems are schools in which the principal and the administration totally refuse any help at all, don't allow the word *suicide* to be mentioned, and refuse to acknowledge that anyone dies of suicide.

Q: My colleague and I have gone into 18 schools in the last 3 years to consult after a suicide. At the beginning we certainly made a lot of mistakes. We now do 98% of what has been described by the panelists. I'd like to comment, to fine-tune two issues. First, I think there needs to be even more emphasis on the enormous pain and distress the school *staff* is feeling in response to the suicide. In terms of priority, indeed, as Dr. Meeks has noted, we must pay primary attention to making sure that other kids are safe. I think a very effective way of doing that is also to address the needs of the school staff. We view the entire school as a survivor. The same kind of dynamics affects family members, peers, and mental health professionals. All members of the community system are going to be reactive when someone in our system commits suicide. By addressing the needs of staff survivors, they can then go on to model the work that needs to be done with the students.

Second, I'd like to say something about the question of the consultant. If I understand Dr. Meeks's comment, he had a preference for the consultant to be an insider, someone identified as being part of the school. I certainly agree. The outside consultant typically is bombarded with all kinds of hostility and all kinds of resistance and distrust. On the other hand, there is a problem when the consultant is an insider. First of all, as an insider, you are a survivor as well. It is a tenet of practice that a therapist who is a survivor of a patient's death should try not to do postvention with the decendent's family. I believe that a consultant who is very closely associated with the school is going to have those same survivor dynamics. The other advantage of being an outsider is that at times you bring legitimacy: as an outsider, you aren't feeling guilty or responsible for the suicide; therefore, you can lend support to the administration, you can lend support in dealing with the media, you can lend support in dealing with parents.

A (Meeks): As a point of clarification, I really was not suggesting that the consultant be an insider but rather that there be an insider who is the coordinator, who brings in the consultant and then pulls together the insider operation. Your point about whether somebody can do that effectively and deal with what he or she has just gone through is very well taken.

Q: I served as a consultant to Bergenfield after the four suicides there in 1987. Bergenfield was very different from any other school system with which I have worked. The anger, grief, guilt, blame, and scapegoating were magnified beyond imagination. As consultants, it was very difficult to remain objective in that emotional climate. We had looked at the video clips of the school meeting that followed the cluster in Omaha, Nebraska. They had a large, very emotional group meeting after the suicides there. When we went to Bergenfield, they had a large group meeting already planned and scheduled. There was no way that they could cancel that meeting. We did encourage them to keep the TV cameras out of the meeting, and I think that was important. But one of the mistakes that occurred was that we underestimated the power of the group process occurring in a large group meeting. We needed to make announcements about walk-in centers, hotlines, and available emergency services but were overwhelmed by that group process. People needed to talk. The atmosphere was too charged. Emotions were high; there was a lot of scapegoating and blaming. I strongly advise the use of small group sessions in order to let people talk.

Second, on a more personal note, I am a survivor of suicide. I lost a teenage brother to suicide 14 years ago. I am therefore sensitized to survivor issues. Because Bergenfield was such a newsworthy event, the families of those victims were traumatized beyond belief. A year after the Bergenfield deaths, one of the siblings came home to find a TV camera on the front lawn. He immediately became worried that somebody else in his family had died. I cannot emphasize enough how important it is for us to sensitize the media, to minimize the stress and trauma that continues to be visited on these families.

A (Cantor): Two points: (1) Even if circumstances demand large group meetings, kids should immediately return to small groups where they can discuss and process what they have learned; and (2) as for media, my experience tells me to "just say no." If somebody calls, and, as has happened, asks me to do a television show to mark the anniversary of the Bergenfield suicides, I refuse. I don't think that this is productive for the community or anybody else. I tell them that if they would like to do a television show on warning signs, listening techniques, what parents should know if there is a crisis, and so on, I would be happy to participate. But if they are going to show the janitor wiping up the blood in the classroom from a suicide a year ago, I don't want to be a part of it. Just say no.

A (Meeks): As far as professionals are concerned, I would agree with Dr. Cantor's comment about the media. Indeed, I get many calls to which I also say no. Controlling the media's access to the family is different; it is basically a political process. What kind of muscle can be brought to bear on them for what is clearly irresponsible journalism? You try to make contacts, to figure out if somebody knows the guy who owns the paper or the TV station or whatever and you squeeze. That's a political world.

A (O'Carroll): The Center for Disease Control's *Morbidity and Mortality Weekly Report* published a story of a cluster that occurred when four teenagers committed suicide in a car by carbon monoxide in a community in New Jersey. It doesn't take much research to figure out what town that is; it is the policy of the Centers for Disease Control publications never to discuss a particular community or even recognize by name that we are discussing a community. If you have worked in community X, someone may call and say, "I know you have worked for community X. Why did that community go bad?" I think the best thing to say is "I never agreed to talk about my experiences in any particular community, but I have worked with this problem and this is what I think." I think we ought to get out of the habit of saying, "Gosh, in Los Angeles it seemed to be this and outside Westchester it was this." Those identifiers don't add anything to our insights as clinicians or consultants. I think we should get away from naming names.

Audience Comment: One thing that we found in our area is that once you have done a program that has been well received by a superintendent or a school system, it is extremely helpful to have them as your advocate with other superintendents and school boards. Their efforts cut down a tremendous amount of our time trying to "sell the program," and they reassure many people that this is the best way to go. It has been extremely effective. The same superintendents and principals who have had good experiences with the suicide-awareness program have also made themselves available to talk to the media when the media want an illustration of a school system. So we have a handout at this point naming about 12 people who are available to either educators or to the media to speak regarding prevention efforts only.

Audience Comment: In trying to figure out how to mitigate contagion, we have to ask what spreads contagion. We have done some experimental research on contagion, and our clinical experience suggests that the avenue by which contagion spreads is a "high affective environment"—an emotion-laden, highly charged environment. Emotions are contagious. So what we want to try to figure out is not whether we do or don't talk about suicide but rather *how* we talk about it, *how* we educate about it, and *how* we can do that in a way that Otto Keinberg calls "technical neutrality," that is, without the powerful affective component that feeds contagion.

O'Carroll: It is notable how similar the recommendations made by the panelists in response to this case were to those by a work group[1] convened in November 1987 to develop a community response plan for suicide

---

[1]The workshop for developing these recommendations was jointly sponsored by the New Jersey State Department of Health and the Centers for Disease Control on November 16–17, 1987, in Newark, New Jersey. Participants in that workshop included persons who had played key roles in community responses to nine different suicide clusters. They were from a variety of different sectors, including education, medicine, local government, community mental health, local crisis centers, and state public health and mental health. Also participating in this workshop were representatives from the National Institute of Mental Health, the Indian Health Service, the American Association of Suicidology, and the Association of State and Territorial Health Officials.

TABLE 2.1. **CDC Recommendations for a Community Plan for the Prevention and Containment of Suicide Clusters**

1. A community should review these recommendations and develop its own response *before* the onset of a suicide cluster.
2. The response to the crisis should involve all concerned sectors of the community and should be coordinated by (a) the coordinating committee, which manages the day-to-day response to the crisis, and (b) the host agency, whose responsibilities would include "housing" the plan, monitoring the incidence of suicide, and calling meetings of the coordinating committee when necessary.
3. The relevant community resources should be identified.
4. The response plan should be implemented under either of the following two conditions: (a) when a suicide cluster occurs in the community, or (b) when one or more deaths from trauma occur in the community, especially among adolescents or young adults, which may potentially influence others to attempt or complete suicide.
5. If the response plan is to be implemented, the first step should be to contact and prepare those groups who will play key roles in the first days of the response.
6. The response should be conducted in a manner that avoids glorification of the suicide victims and minimizes sensationalism.
7. Persons who may be at high risk of suicide should be identified and have at least one screening interview with a trained counselor; these persons should be referred for further counseling or other services as needed.
8. A timely flow of accurate, appropriate information should be provided to the media.
9. Elements in the environment that might increase the likelihood of further suicides or suicide attempts should be identified and changed.
10. Long-term issues suggested by the nature of the suicide cluster should be addressed.

clusters. That work group also made several additonal recommendations (Table 2.1). The recommendations from that workshop were published by the Centers for Disease Control in August 1988 (CDC, 1988) and have already been used by a number of community leaders in public health, mental health, education, and other fields in responding to suicide clusters.

There appears, therefore, to be at least a general consensus on how best to respond to suicide clusters among those who have responded to such clusters and others who work in suicide prevention. More research is needed, however, to answer a number of important questions. For example, are there particular risk factors for cluster suicide, as opposed to suicide in general, that would help us identify which persons were at highest risk of committing suicide in the context of a cluster? Is there any way to anticipate (and thus prevent) suicide clusters? More specifically, can we characterize which traumatic deaths among adolescents or young adults are most likely to instigate a suicide cluster? Finally, how can we evaluate whether the recommendations made by the AAS panelists and the New Jersey work group are effective in preventing cluster suicides? Answers to these questions would be of immediate relevance to the prevention and control of suicide clusters. In the meantime, the collective experience represented by the AAS panelists and by members of the New Jersey work group, coupled with our present scientific understanding of risk factors for suicide, should guide us in responding to suicide clusters.

REFERENCES

Bakwin, H. (1957). Suicide in children and adolescents. *Journal of Pediatrics, 50,* 749–769.

Baron, J. N., & Reiss, P. C. (1985). Same time, next year: Aggregate analyses of the mass media and violent behavior. *American Sociological Review, 50,* 347–363.

Berman, A. L. (1988). Fictional depiction of suicide in television films and imitative effects. *American Journal of Psychiatry, 145,* 982–986.

Bunch, J. G., Barraclough, B., Nelson, B., & Sainsbury, P. (1971). Suicide following bereavement of parents. *Social Psychiatry, 6,* 193–199.

Cain, A. C., & Fast, I. (1972). The legacy of suicide: Observations on the pathogenic impact of suicide on marital partners. In A. C. Cain (Ed.), *Survivors of suicide* (pp. 145–154). Springfield, IL: Charles C. Thomas.

Centers for Disease Control. (1988). CDC recommendations for a community plan for the prevention and containment of suicide clusters. *Morbidity and Mortality Weekly Report, 37* (Suppl. S-6), 1–12.

Davidson, L., & Gould, M. S. (1989). Contagion as a risk factor for youth suicide. In U.S. Department of Health and Human Services (Ed.), *Report of the Secretary's Task Force on Youth Suicide: Risk factors for youth suicide* vol. 2, pp. 88–109). Publication (ADM) 89-1622. Washington, DC: U.S. Department of Health and Human Services.

Gould, M. S., & Shaffer, D. (1986). The impact of suicide in television movies: Evidence of imitation. *New England Journal of Medicine, 315,* 690–694.

Gould, M.S., Wallenstein, S., & Davidson, L. (1989). Suicide clusters: A critical review. *Suicide and Life-threatening Behavior, 19,* 17–29.

Gould, M. S., Wallenstein, S., & Kleinman, M. (1987). *A study of time-space clustering of suicide: Final report* (Contract No. RFP 200-85-0834). Atlanta: Centers for Disease Control.

Hagin, A. D. (1986). Understanding suicide. In S. Daniels & D. Pass (Eds.), *Suicide prevention and caregiving* (pp. 9–11). Milwaukee, WI: National Funeral Directors Association.

Hankoff, L. D. (1961). An epidemic of attempted suicide. *Comprehensive Psychiatry, 2,* 294–298.

Kessler, R. D., & Stipp, H. (1984). The impact of fictional television suicide stories on U.S. fatalities: A replication. *American Journal of Sociology, 90* 151–167.

Phillips, D. P., & Carstensen L. L. (1986). Clustering of teenage suicides after television news stories about suicide. *New England Journal of Medicine, 315,* 685–689.

Phillips, D. P., & Paight, D. J. (1987). The impact of televised movies about suicide: A replicative study. *New England Journal of Medicine, 317,* 809–811.

Pynoos, R. S., & Eth, S. (1985). Children traumatized by witnessing acts of personal violence: Homicide, rape, or suicide behavior. In S. Eth & R. S. Pynoos (Eds.), *Post-traumatic stress disorder in children* (pp. 17–43). Washington, DC: American Psychiatric Association.

Pynoos, R. S., Frederick, C., Nader, K., Arroyo, W., Steinberg, A., Eth, S., Nunez, F., & Fairbanks, L. (1987). Life threat and posttraumatic stress in school-age children. *Archives of General Psychiatry, 44,* 1057–1063.

Robbins, D., & Conroy, R. D. (1983). A cluster of adolescent suicide attempts: Is suicide contagious? *Journal of Adolescent Health Care, 3,* 253–255.

Ward, J. A., & Fox, J. (1977). A suicide epidemic on an Indian reserve. *Canadian Psychiatric Association Journal, 22,* 423–426.

3

Suicide Prevention: Community Services

The first known suicide prevention program in the United States was the National Save-A-Life League, founded in New York City in 1906. However, it was not until the late 1950s, with the establishment of the Los Angeles Suicide Prevention Center, that the modern crisis service, centered around the innovative melding of the telephone and the trained paraprofessional volunteer, came into being. With this development came new definitions and patterns of service delivery. At once, potential clients had 24-hour access to immediate support and referral. They could remain anonymous (as could the help-giver), never have to leave home, and receive free mental health services under their control rather than that of an agency or professional.

The federal government's support of the community mental health movement, mandating and funding 24-hour services (*Action for Mental Health*, 1961), gave impetus to the growth of crisis intervention services within established mental health agencies throughout the 1960s; and the relatively concurrent movements of volunteerism and countercultural activism throughout the Vietnam era in the United States spurred a rapid proliferation of services and programs lasting well into the mid-1970s. In more recent years, many programs have faced funding crises and great competition for available volunteers. Lacking effective leadership, these programs have folded. Others have moved toward providing specialized services, meeting the needs of teens or rape victims, battered spouses or runaways. As of late 1988, the American Association of Suicidology (AAS) listed 623 programs in its *Directory of Suicide Prevention Centers and Crisis Intervention Agencies in the United States*,[1] a number believed to be quite conservative as it excluded services operating at less than 24-hour or overnight service delivery and highly specialized phone lines.

In 1976 the AAS pioneered the establishment of standards for crisis services by launching a program for certification, in which crisis centers are

---

[1]This directory is available from the American Association of Suicidology, 2459 So. Ash, Denver, CO 80222.

evaluated through site visits according to predefined minimum standards in seven areas: administration, training, service delivery, suicide prevention services, ethical issues, community integration, and program evaluation. As a check on the effectiveness and service potential of these often untraditional programs, certification procedures allow for external validation of programs relative to their own and generally accepted goals and community needs. Today, however, only 53 of the programs listed above have been certified.

Inherent in these changes in the last two decades is an increased focus on and concern with service effectiveness. Studies evaluating the effectiveness of crisis services and hotlines have been reviewed recently by Shaffer and his colleagues (Shaffer, Garland, Gould, Fisher, & Trautman, 1988), who concluded that these services have demonstrated only "limited impact" (p. 682). Explaining these findings, Shaffer et al. offer two possible reasons:

1. The suicide-prone population, those at greater risk, tend not to use a telephone service. For example, older male alcoholics generally are not represented among profiles of callers to a hotline. Although this criticism is true in terms of maximum impact, the more significant question pertains to the success of interventions with those who do utilize such services, for example, young female callers.

2. The quality of advice and information given, reflecting the quality of training received, is generally poor and leads to low levels of compliance. Inherent in this criticism are questions of how much training should be given to nonprofessionals to impart a quality of professionalism to their skills in handling difficult problems and clients. Compliance also may be a function of how much outreach a service provides, that is, the service's ability to mobilize its and/or the community's resources to implement an action plan once a problem definition calls for such intervention.

Thus, whereas suicide prevention has been the primary goal and impetus for the development of 24-hour crisis centers, dealing with the problems posed by the suicidal client may be the most questionable of the crisis center's strengths. The following case illustrates well the myriad of issues and problems faced by a hotline service in dealing with a severely disturbed suicidal clilent who is representative of frequent clients of such a program.

CASE STUDY: THE CRISIS CENTER

Editor's note: The following descriptive notes summarize the contact between the client-caller and the crisis worker as well as the follow-up interactions.

Case Description

Female adolescent caller to 24-hour crisis line threatened suicide. Crisis center notified of client's death by police within 24 hours of call.

Details of Crisis Call

Seventeen-year-old white female called from local hotel in early morning. Reported unwanted pregnancy; the father reported to be her black boyfriend. Struggling with issue of abortion or having the baby.

Threatened suicide by cutting wrist. Ambivalence verbalized. Thoughts of suicide equated to aborting the baby. Wanted to have baby (and would run away to another state upon delivery) despite suggestions of friends and boyfriend to have an abortion. Reported having contacted favorite teacher prior to contacting crisis line.

Client had history of previous attempts. Discharged from psychiatric hospital (1 year ago) and reported lessons learned there as being in conflict with her suicidal thoughts.

Client abruptly terminated after 1 hour on telephone. Counselor reported client had little self-awareness, kept distance, did not accept counselor's warmth, "not an easy connection."

Contact with Police

Client found dead in hotel room midmorning. Hotel released telephone numbers of local calls made by client, and crisis center was listed. Police reported investigating case as homicide or suicide. Reported client exsanguinated due to slash on arm and that she and boyfriend had been arguing prior to her death.

Contact with Mother

Unsolicited by crisis center, client's mother contacted business office within 3 days of suicide about memorial contributions. She was unaware of daughter's contact with crisis center.

Mother reported relief as daughter's psychiatric treatment, suicide threats, and recent troublesome behavior were complicated, scary, and confusing. Mother verbalized concern for a close male friend of the client's who was treated in same hospital at same time. Reported conflict between this male and client's boyfriend in hours prior to client's suicide.

Feared a suicide pact and was in communication with his parents. Mother willing and able to participate in SOS (Survivors of Suicide) group.

Contact with Medical Examiner

Approached by crisis center to review the case and center's participation with client. Reported carvings and initialing on body: two to three cuts to arm prior to slashing radial artery from which client bled to death. Reported hotel towel wrapped around arm.

Reported three suicide notes found, addressed to several male figures. Long history of unsatisfying love relationships.

Hotel room in disarray, cluttered with debris: ambivalence evident. Investigated relationships between boyfriend, client, and male friend prior to death.

Death ruled suicide. Toxicology analyses reported equivalent of one drink in body.

Issues for Crisis Centers

On the basis of this case, the following questions were addressed to the panel of consultants:

How is the working relationship with a client established by a telephone counselor?
How are incapacities to establish a relationship assessed by a counselor?
How are risk assessments completed?
What variables (risk factors) are explored and emphasized?
What is the relationship between a center's understanding of suicidal risk and its intervention tactics?
What position is appropriate and ethical for a center to take relative to confidentiality of a deceased client's records and contacts by external agencies and/or family?
How does a center debrief the suicide of a caller/client with volunteer counselors, staff, and the external agents (if necessary or demanded)?

COMMENTARY

Zigfrids Stelmachers:

Perhaps the cornerstone of rapport building is being attuned to the patient's agenda. This presumes the ability to listen between the lines, to detect major themes, and to respond to the caller's pain and suffering.

It also means assigning a lower priority to one's own agenda, which is typically based on a need for various types of information. At the very least, the counselor's agenda has to be flexibly intertwined with that of the caller. Everyone seems to know and endorse the value of listening, but surprisingly few do it well. Our anxieties and needs for structure interfere with empathetic listening. So do premature attempts to fix and solve problems before one has reached a thorough enough understanding of the caller. It is good to remember that sometimes doing less is more, therapeutically speaking. Crisis intervention seems to attract people with an activist orientation, which can often be counterproductive to such listening. Too often phone counselors proceed directly from data gathering to problem solving, with little psychological intervention in between. At the most basic level, all one has to do is match the caller's typical "need to talk to someone" with the counselor's willingness to listen and receive the message, without cluttering up the latter with one's own garbage.

In this particular case, it is not clear from the information provided whether we are dealing with the caller's or the counselor's "incapacity." After all, the client did reach out and spent a whole hour on the phone. This certainly reveals at least moderate motivation to establish and maintain contact. However, this brings up a programmatic question that is surrounded by a fair degree of controversy: the merits of phone versus face-to-face counseling.

After 4 years of administering a suicide hotline and 17 years of directing a comprehensive crisis intervention center, there is no doubt in my mind that phone counseling has serious limitations, such as the absence of visual cues and too little control of the situation on the counselor's part. Many emergent clinical dispositions can be achieved more readily in a face-to-face situation. For instance, in this particular case, the likelihood of an abrupt termination of contact could have been easily avoided. It is for good reason that the AAS's certification standards give programs credit for walk-in capability. In my opinion, phones are excellent vehicles for easy and prompt access but a poor medium for the actual intervention, particularly if the intervention involves more than verbal interaction.

Risk Assessment

In the situation depicted, it is not clear at all if *any* suicide risk assessment was done! Were any risk rating scales used? Was a global risk rating assigned? There is no evidence of any *clinical* evaluation of suicidal signs and symptoms, no attention paid to diagnostic issues, especially symptoms of depression and hopelessness. And this despite a whole hour's worth of phone contact.

Looking over the information provided, the following items would seem to go with lower risk: caller is female, young, the method planned not typically lethal. There is evidence of ambivalence, motivation to seek help, and good experience with previous treatment. Also, she maintains contact with a counselor for an hour.

Factors indicative of elevated suicide risk are history of suicide attempts, previous psychiatric hospitalization, significant stressors (unwanted pregnancy, conflict over abortion versus having the baby), keeping emotional distance from the counselor, little self-awareness, and abrupt termination. Above all, for imminent risk, the fact that the girl called from a hotel during the early hours of the morning would seem a very ominous sign.

I gave the case vignette to seven experienced crisis counselors asking them to assign a suicide risk. Results: all of them felt that the risk was high for a suicide *attempt*; five gave a "moderate" rating for short-term risk, and two gave a "moderate high" rating for completed suicide.

It should be better understood that assessing a person's suicide risk is not the same as predicting specific suicidal behaviors. The rating merely assigns the individual to a particular risk group. As we know, the great majority of individuals in even the highest risk groups currently measurable by the available instruments will not commit suicide; and those who do may commit suicide many years later. Aside from the base-rate problem, there is the issue of precipitating event and available opportunity, neither of which we typically have much control over.

Although the scores derived from empirically constructed rating scales seem to be relatively reliable across raters, this is less true of global subjective judgments of suicide risk. In an actual clinical setting, one would hardly ever rely entirely on such scores. Other factors not contained in the rating scale will always play a significant role and introduce a fair amount of subjectivity. And yet these unreliable global judgments have to be connected with intervention strategies. Moreover, the latter are as situation- and setting-specific as are the ratings themselves. Certain interventions are simply not possible in a given center (again, the limitations of a hotline are quite apparent).

In this particular case, did the counselor obtain the caller's name, address, and phone number? Some centers used to (perhaps still do) emphasize the desirability of anonymity of the caller, the intent being to encourage the client to freely share confidences. This, I believe, is a serious error, at least in cases of imminent suicide risk. In this case, for instance, such information would have been invaluable for initiating rescue.

Short of such information, tracing the phone call could have been considered, but it is not clear if this was done. (One hour might have been enough for a trace to succeed.)

If prevention of suicide is the ultimate goal of a center—as distinct from confidential counseling of troubled and suicidal people—there has to be programmatic capacity for swift and vigorous, even involuntary, intervention. Clinical situations and the estimated levels of suicide risk need to be connected with proposed interventions. Ideally, such interventions have to encompass the whole range from least to most restrictive and be available—either directly by the center itself or through some arrangement with an outside agency.

Confidentiality

The issue of what position a center should take relative to confidentiality of a deceased client's records is basically a legal as much as an ethical question. In Minnesota it is quite clearly spelled out in the Data Privacy Act. The records are available to the "next of kin" only. If other family members or agencies want to obtain the records, permission must be obtained from the next of kin.

From my own experience and clinical reports in the literature (Litman, 1982) it certainly seems wise to share available information about the deceased with the family. Ironically, fear of litigation may lead to stonewalling relatives' requests for information and unwittingly lead to the very thing one is trying to avoid. Not only do the relatives have the right to such information, but there is plenty of clinical evidence that information about the deceased is a therapeutic ingredient in the grief process. Treating the survivors *clinically* rather than *administratively* is therapeutically proper and may avoid lawsuits in addition.

Debriefing

Concerning the question of how a center debriefs its staff after a caller/client suicide, I believe all mental health programs, professionals, and volunteers have the obligation to review all suicides and life-threatening suicide attempts, especially if they occur shortly after the contact with the program. The purpose is threefold: for learning, corrective action, and catharsis. It may not be possible, however, to achieve these goals within the same meeting. Peer review and administrative review can be accomplished simultaneously if done with caution and sensitivity. If records of such reviews are kept, one needs to check out their legal status in case of a future lawsuit (if some negligence is revealed in the review process). To ensure a frank discussion of the case, it is advisable legally to protect the record from possible subpoena.

Mary Smith:

I will address the case study from the telephone counselor's perspective, taking into account only the information that was available to the counselor as a result of telephone contact with the caller. This will necessarily exclude information available in the case study that was provided by other sources following the call. My reason for proceeding in this way is to help clarify the role and the responsibility of a telephone counselor in the case of a suicide call. At the end of my presentation I shall ask a number of questions regarding the call and the counselor's assessment of the call, which I hope will stimulate further thought and discussion.

Establishing a Working Relationship

How does the counselor establish a working relationship with this caller? I suggest that such a relationship begins with the voice quality used throughout the call. From the very beginning, the counselor should sound calm and comfortable in the conversation, strong and capable in the counselor role yet gentle with the caller's feelings. The relationship will develop positively in direct proportion to the counselor's listening skills. Second, active listening—hearing feelings as well as words and allowing them to create a basis for further exploration—is essential to establishing rapport with the caller. A third quality important for establishing the necessary rapport with a caller is acceptance. In this case the caller *is* who she is and *feels* as she feels, and the counselor needs to recognize and accept *that person* with *those feelings* at *that time* even though the person or feelings might not be acceptable to the counselor outside the call. It is important to recognize that accepting the feelings of the caller does not mean that one is accepting the caller's assessment of the circumstances surrounding her feelings or the caller's judgment of the best means of addressing those feelings or of changing them. Specifically, in this case, the young woman may well have been feeling helpless in the face of her pregnancy and hopeless about finding someone who would support and encourage her in her desire to keep the baby; she may even have felt worthless as a human being because of her situation, all of which the counselor could respond to with acceptance and understanding. To the caller such circumstances and feelings may add up to suicide as a solution, but the counselor does *not* need to accept that at face value. The caller is expressing ideation based on her feelings, and the counselor's role is to explore those feelings and help the caller identify alternative, life-embracing options. In this case, the caller verbalized ambivalence regarding her suicidal intentions. It would be important for the counselor to explore that ambivalence as deeply as possible and attempt to build on the life-affirming side of that spectrum.

Assessing Difficult Relationship Connections

With the foregoing guidelines for establishing a working relationship with a caller in mind, how might a counselor assess a lack of capacity for establishing such rapport? The counselor in this case study reported that the client "kept distance, did not accept the counselor's warmth, and was not an easy connection." The most blatant evidence of lack of relationship is a caller hanging up abruptly after a limited number of exchanges or the caller saying that the counselor is not able to help, with or without giving reasons, and then hanging up. Some of the reasons might be the sex of the counselor, the age of the counselor as deduced by the caller, some undesired answer to a question, or the perception by the caller that the counselor cannot or will not understand the problem.

A third kind of failure occurs when the caller will not or cannot enter into open give-and-take conversation with the counselor but insists on maintaining control of all subject matter. An example of this might be an exchange similar to the following:

> *Caller:* I told you before; I'm going to kill myself!
> *Counselor:* Have you decided *how* you are going to do that?
> *Caller:* What difference does that make? I'll be dead no matter how I do it.
> *Counselor:* I'll tell you the truth; it makes a big difference to me because I would like to help you look at other options than death to end your pain.
> *Caller:* What do you mean, "pain"? I'm not injured or sick or anything.

A great deal of patience and sensitivity is required for the caller in this kind of attacking–defending state of mind to finally give up defending and begin sharing further information about the life events that are involved with the suicidal thoughts.

A working relationship sometimes is hindered by the mental state of the caller. Although reliable psychiatric assessment is certainly not expected or indeed possible by a nonprofessional on the phone, telephone counselors can be trained to recognize signs of mental illness that limit a caller's ability to enter into helpful relationships. If there is a flat affect, if the caller reports concerns without emotion shown in the voice or in the choice of words, and/or if the caller changes the subject from one concern to another, and all efforts to focus on a single problem are met with failure, it is possible that there is a psychiatric problem inhibiting that particular call. Counselors should be aware of this possibility and know that in such cases the usual procedures will not be very effective. Probably the best approach is for the counselor to invest energy in pursuing and supporting specific and well-defined options with the caller. The statement made in the case study that the client "had little self-awareness" may have been an indicator of such a situation, especially since it was known that the caller had previously spent time in a psychiatric hospital. I can't help wondering if the counselor in this case may not have expected more from the relationship with the caller than was possible, given the circumstances.

Risk Assessment

The use of a good risk assessment instrument is very important—I would say essential—to effective handling of a suicide call. I find myself reaching for my center's blue lethality sheet just as soon as I begin to even suspect suicidal ideation or intent. I can always discard the sheet if it develops that the caller is only using suicide talk in the mistaken belief that that's the only way or the best way to gain my attention. In the meantime I'm guided by my lethality sheet in exploring critical specifics that will lead to a more valid assessment and will be a basis, in consultation, for pursuing intervention steps.

Our lethality sheet has three functions: to assess the immediate condition of the caller, to help create a plan of action, and to be useful in follow-up. Space is provided for all pertinent demographic information and the listing of significant others. I want to emphasize that even when I have not sensed the possible need for utilizing this sheet I make it a practice to write down any name I hear, any place mentioned, or any specific information gleaned in *any* call I handle. Sometimes it can be very helpful to have a specific name or place that was mentioned only casually by the caller.

The sheet continues with a number of items addressing lethality. These items include the suicide plan, the time planned, the method, the availability of the means, the location of the caller and/or the execution of the plan, the possibility of intervention. It follows with circumstances of the caller's life that would be expected to affect a suicidal decision. These factors include recent loss, being a survivor of suicide, past suicide attempts, psychiatric treatment and/or hospitalizations and any current medication, the availability of any therapist involved with the caller, and mood. Each of these categories is rated as to low, medium, or high levels of intensity, and one can come to a rather clear picture of the level of lethality by reviewing the checks in each of the categories. At Crisis Hotline the rule of thumb for using this information is that the higher the risk, the sooner and the more necessary it is for a volunteer to seek consultation with staff and the more probable that intervention steps will be taken. Therefore, it is important for me to establish an estimated level of lethality as soon as possible.

Relating this to the case study presented, there were lots of different pieces of specific information that I would want to get from the caller as soon as possible, including specifics about all of the potential resources for intervention available to her and to me as counselor.

Suicidal Risk and Intervention Tactics

What is the relationship between a center's understanding of suicidal risk and its intervention tactics? As has been stated, in general practice, the higher the risk of completion of suicide, the more intervention steps are undertaken. And the sooner the high-risk factors are communicated from the caller to the counselor, or solicited by the counselor from the caller, the sooner such steps can begin. All specific pieces of information are important, and any one may be critical in intervention. Possible avenues available for intervention in this case would include contacting the hotel desk if the name of the hotel has been obtained from the caller and contacting family members, the boyfriend or other friends, the teacher mentioned, and any of the therapists the caller had seen or the hospital where she'd been treated. The possibility of success with any of these interventions depends on the counselor's ability to solicit specific information from the caller. If the caller's exact location is not obtained, then a telephone trace on the call might be initiated while the call continues. At some point the police might be called if the location of the caller can be ascertained.

In my experience, it is not my prerogative as a volunteer counselor to make the decision as to when to intervene in a suicide call and through whom to seek intervention, and I am glad that is the case. I have available to me and am expected to use the help of trained professional staff persons who *must* be contacted before any third-party call is made. Such staff persons may rely heavily on my input and undoubtedly will expect assessment data from the lethality sheet to be as complete as possible. In this case, I would have made contact with our on-call staff person as early into the call as I had perceived that the caller had a suicidal plan and that the level of lethality appeared to be high. Because it is very easy for telephone counselors, especially unseasoned ones, to get caught up in the emotions of a call and not use their best judgment at such a time, I feel that consultation is extremely important. In addition, a crisis center's credibility depends on the response it solicits from individuals, therapists, doctors, police, ambulance services, telephone company personnel, and others. So the decisions as to how, when, and through whom to intervene is best made by professional consultants or by others specifically trained in this aspect of crisis work. In the event that the counselor on duty is empowered to intervene without benefit of consultation, as is the case in some crisis centers, then well-defined guidelines for deciding when and through what channels to intervene are essential to effective operation.

Confidentiality of Client Records

The question of confidentiality and the appropriate and ethical position for a center to take relative to clients' records is one of extreme importance. However, decisions regarding confidentiality of records are the responsibility of a center's board or other governing body. I am committed as a telephone counselor to keep confidential *all* that I hear on the phone line, even items that might become news headlines. As a former board president, I recognize that there are many dimensions to the issue of disclosure, including state laws requiring the reporting of certain events. This is an area in which it would be valuable for those interested and concerned to develop appropriate and detailed guidelines for use by centers and volunteers.

Debriefing

Debriefing after a suicide call is critical for the counselor's support and mental health, for continued functioning on the phones, for skill development and growth, and for a continuing trusting working relationship with any supervision personnel.

First, in a serious call in which the caller terminates the call abruptly, the counselor is left feeling deserted and with more than a measure of unfinished business. In a suicide call, the counselor will feel considerable anxiety as well. In our center, there typically are other counselors available to listen. I will let it be known that I need to discuss the call and will share my feelings and concerns along with details of the call. Our volunteer counselors are trained to listen and be supportive in such cases; we are also trained to try to be aware of the seriousness of fellow-workers' calls in progress so that we can more easily facilitate debriefing when a "heavy" call is finished. I may be encouraged by my fellow volunteer to discuss the problems further with the staff member on call. We have a staff member on call 24 hours a day.

In the case presented, the debriefing is going to be even more traumatic than usual because the counselor is going to be faced with the fact of a completed suicide following his or her talk with the caller. I am grateful that this has never happened to me in more than 17 years on the phones. However, it could happen tomorrow. I know and accept it in my thinking as part of my own approach to participating in this kind of volunteer service. I can only do so much in any given situation; I am not responsible for the actions of a telephone caller; I *am* responsible for developing the best possible telephone counseling and intervention skills and for doing my best to couple those skills with a caring concern for another human being. I need to be reminded frequently that recognizing such limitations of my role and my responsibilities is essential for effective functioning on the line. If this case call had been mine, I would need to hear from my supervisors that *I* did not make the decision for suicide— the caller did; that I had spent an hour with her attempting to find alternatives to that decision to die; that it was not known what happened between her call and her death, a time period over which I had absolutely no control. With these kinds of supportive messages in my head, I could then be led to review the call, to look carefully at various aspects of the information I had gleaned from the caller, and to assess with my supervisor the strengths and weaknesses of my assumptions and my decisions. I probably would also need reassurance over the next several weeks that I could indeed handle future suicide calls and that in all probability this very difficult experience would help me to be an even better telephone counselor because of what I had learned.

Because of the seeming public nature of this case, the debriefing would need to extend to other volunteers, to staff, and to board members, who might have read in the papers that the victim had called the crisis center before her suicide. In a center in which all board members, staff, and volunteers are dedicated to *preventing* suicide, a completed suicide occurring after a call to the center could lead to universal feelings of failure. For that reason it is very important to review each group's specific role, responsibilities, *and* limitations in relation to prevention. It is important to recognize both strengths and weaknesses in general procedures and in the specific case at hand and to discuss avenues for growth and improvement in all possible areas of functioning. It might be valuable to obtain the help of an outside staff consultant to lead such debriefings at the board and staff levels.

Questions

I would like to propose several questions among dozens I found myself asking as I studied the information given about this call.

1. What kind of affect was the counselor perceiving in the caller at different times within the call? Were there any changes in that affect, or was it flat throughout?
2. What was the content of the call to the teacher? Was the teacher supportive of the caller, or did it result in further feelings of alienation?
3. Did the counselor explore with the caller the resources available to the caller to pursue her stated desire to have the baby and move to another state, perhaps as a viable alternative to her suicide plan?
4. If one were to ask the counselor what characteristics of the call contributed to her assessment of it as a "difficult connection," what would the counselor say? Is it possible that the counselor was feeling an

unrealistic amount of responsibility for the caller's suicide and that he or she "should" have been able to prevent it and therefore was trying to justify failure with the reflective assessment?

5. Did the counselor have consultation resources available during the call? If so, was their use considered at any point prior to the end of the call? If not, did the counselor consider intervention procedures along the way?

6. Was there an audible interruption prior to termination of the call? What were the caller's parting words? What was her mood at termination?

As you readily can see, there are many questions left unanswered. These questions suggest areas for exploration by the crisis counselor. They also indicate the scope of expertise in telephone intervention that such a counselor needs to develop through training and experience. There will always be some unanswered questions following a telephone intervention. For this one very important reason, counselors answering such calls should be mature individuals with a strong sense of their own self-worth, well trained in an understanding of their job and in their limitations in meeting the needs of callers.

COMMENTARY

James Wells:

I am going to examine this case from the perspective of the American Association of Suicidology's Certification Committee. The American Association of Suicidology is the standard-setting body for crisis centers. As past chief certification examiner, it is difficult for me to read this case without evaluating the functioning of the crisis center in question vis-à-vis the *Certification Standards Manual.*

The seven areas covered by the *Standards* are administration, training procedures, general service delivery, services in life-threatening crises, ethical issues, community integration, and program evaluation. I will address each separately, in relation to this case.

Administration

I suspect that the center in this case would have fared adequately in the area of administration. The mother of the deceased client contacted the *business office,* which implies at least some part-time paid staff and perhaps a business line separate from the crisis line. I wonder about the adequacy of the physical setting. Did the crisis worker receive this early morning call at home or through a telephone switching device?

Training Procedures

One question that arises is whether there was a determination, during the screening, selection, and training of the crisis worker, that this person could work uninfluenced by prejudices. In the case presented, there was room for attitudes about "illegitimate" pregnancy, abortion, people with a history of psychiatric hospitalizations, and racial issues, each of which might have obscured purely clinical considerations. Other important questions, germane to this area of program functioning, include the following:

- Was the counselor up to date in methods of suicide risk assessment?
- Was the training well balanced between the development of knowledge, skills, and attitudes?
- Did the crisis worker have experience role-playing difficult calls?
- Did the crisis worker receive training in policies and procedures?

Service Delivery

In terms of service delivery, it appears that the crisis line operates 24 hours a day. Its capacity for 24-hour outreach is thus the next question raised by this case. Does the center do its own outreach? Does it have an agreement or contract for the service, or does it merely send the police? These considerations, in turn, raise the question of whether there was enough information available to have located the client and also whether the client would have been amenable to face-to-face, walk-in service.

Of particular concern here is the center's policy and practice regarding follow-up on crisis cases. I think that this would have qualified as a "crisis case" by any center's definition. Is this a center that makes no effort to ascertain client identity, or did the worker try to do so and the client refused? What if follow-up information were available and the center had a written policy that all crisis cases would be followed up within 24 hours, or 8 hours, or 4 hours? The fact is that time limits may not adequately address the requirements of an individual case. Is that addressed in the policies? (All of the above assumes that the information needed for follow-up has been properly documented.)

Services in Life-Threatening Crises

One can see that in this case the elements of an assessment of lethality are present. However, one might ask whether the information was collected haphazardly or systematically. A certification examiner would hope to find a specific place on the client's call sheet for recording lethality. With the clarity afforded by hindsight, one also wonders about the center's capability for effecting rescue. What are its policies and procedures? Some centers trace a call at the drop of a hint; others do not or cannot trace calls. There should be a clear relationship between the degree of risk and the institution of rescue procedures. Would this case have warranted a trace?

It is apparent that this center does have a suicide survivor service. I wonder whether outreach efforts would be made to others, for example, the boyfriend, the teacher, and other friends. Also, would the mother have been contacted had she not called the center herself?

Ethical Issues

Among *ethical issues*, confidentiality is most relevant. In this case, the three biggest areas for potential compromise exist with the police, the medical examiner, and the mother. For example, although the police provided helpful information, it is unclear what, if anything, the crisis center shared with them. In a pragmatic sense, what is released to the police sometimes depends more on the nature of the working relationship with them than on the minimum needed to complete the police investigation.

I was surprised that the crisis center approached the medical examiner to review the center's part in the case. The medical examiner may have legal access to the center's records, but he or she needs only the information necessary to determine the mode of death. In this case, the medical examiner apparently already had enough information.

State laws vary as to who may have access to a client's records upon the death of that client. If the client was a minor child, not classified as an emancipated minor, the confidentiality might pass to a parent who is still legal guardian. However, in this case, once the client is deceased, I believe that the center would not have the duty to inform the mother that she had called, although the center might decide to do this, based on a humane, survivor-oriented caring.

If the center had not already done so, the crisis could set the occasion for engaging a lawyer to review the center's ethical standards, policies on confidentiality, and rescue policies, to assure that they are in keeping with local laws.

Community Integration

There are indications that the center may be well integrated into the community. For example, the mother made an unsolicited call about memorial contributions. Also, the police and the medical examiner both seem willing to release details about the death to the center, indicating that it has some credibility in the community. In addition, there is a group for survivors of suicide.

Evaluation

All crisis centers should evaluate their activities. Perhaps one of the things implied when there is a suicide by a client is that the center is dealing with the right population—the one at high risk.

Among the purposes of the psychological autopsy a major one is that of evaluation. I would therefore want to see documentation that a psychological autopsy had occurred. Although I would not expect to see it reflected in the documentation, I would hope that such an autopsy also would provide an opportunity for venting feelings and for staff support.

In the psychological autopsy, I would expect to find documentation of evaluation in the areas of prevention, intervention, and postvention. Questions to be addressed might include the following:

1. Were there lessons from this case that should be included in initial and ongoing training to help other crisis workers in their performance?
2. Are there policies or procedures that should be modified, such as backup, supervision, rescue, follow-up, or anything that will lead to more effective future interventions?
3. After learning of the death, did the crisis worker receive adequate debriefing and support?
4. Was the support immediate enough? Helpful enough? Did it follow written protocol?
5. Did the psychological autopsy occur soon enough to be helpful but still allow enough time for reports and other information to be gathered?
6. Is there documentation of actions taken based on this incident?

When there is a suicidal death shortly after contact with a crisis center, there is another important question to ask: What occurred between the time of the last contact and the time of death? Specific questions to determine this might include the following:

1. Why did the client hang up abruptly after an hour? Was there someone at the door? Did the red light on the hotel phone start blinking, indicating a message?
2. Was the argument with the boyfriend after the crisis call? Was the argument in person or over the phone?
3. Were the telephone numbers of local calls released by the hotel in chronological order? Who are the people she called, and what was said?
4. Was there a reason for the client's slight alteration in suicide plan— from cutting her wrists to slashing her arm and radial artery?

In summary, I have examined this case from the point of view of a certification examiner and, in so doing, have raised more questions than I have answered. However, these questions are meant to provide those who might consider applying for center certification with the flavor of some of the things that a certification examiner might probe for during a site survey.

Questions and Responses

Q: Dr. Stelmachers, you used the phrase "protect from subpoena" when referring to records. What did you mean by that?

A (Stelmachers): The relatives of the suicide may decide that there was negligence or malpractice involved in the suicide prevention efforts and sue the care provider. If it is discovered that records about the suicidal client were kept, the relatives may want to obtain them to see if they contain material damaging to the care provider. They could use the findings of a suicide review to strengthen their case if records were kept and contain critical comments about the care provided to the suicidal patient.

Q: Are you suggesting that the process should be hidden from the legal system in some way?

A (Stelmachers): Yes. Peer review subjected to legal scrutiny would certainly hamper achieving the necessary openness in discussing the case. For instance, if a center institutes some changes in a program following a review, one could argue that the necessity to make improvements ipso facto proves that there must have been something wrong with the care provided in the first place. But that would be counterproductive to encouraging improvements. The courts are usually enlightened and understand that that would stifle change for the better. So the simple fact that improvements were made would not be used by the courts as evidence of some preexisting deficiency in the program.

Q: Certainly, having a written policy regarding suicide cases would protect the center in some way.

A (Stelmachers): There is an additional way to protect a center and its review process. That is by using the center's attorney as part of its review process. Communications between the center/client and attorney may be protected by attorney-client privilege.

Q: I understand that the mother, as survivor, legally has access to the center's records. Would you suggest volunteering that information to the survivor?

A (Stelmachers): I would. Dr. Litman's 1982 article summarized a number of cases and concluded that if relatives are stonewalled— that is, not provided information—anger is aroused and lawsuits provoked. In my experience, it is best to take a clinical approach, to treat survivors like survivors, not potential litigants, to help them with their grief, their guilt, and their need for information.

Q: Ms. Smith, you mentioned that the volunteer should involve the staff at a very early point in any kind of intervention. Do you believe that volunteers' willingness to do just that is a function of the amount of training a center has given them? Second, do you believe that volunteer's response is related to the culture a crisis center is willing to support, that is, setting expectations for volunteer performance, providing supervision, and generally establishing a culture of high-level service and high-level peer and staff support?

A (Smith): I think it has a lot to do with the community and the structure of the crisis center. Houston, the city in which I volunteer, has a population of over 2 million people. It would be very difficult for our center to maintain credibility with the various institutions (e.g., police, rescue squads) if each of our 150 volunteers were empowered to call for a community service whenever he or she felt it necessary. By making the rescue activation a staff decision, it is less likely to be sought in situations where it would be inappropriate or unproductive. Volunteers can be trained to recognize the need for outside intervention during their calls in progress and to practice effective methods of making contact with those empowered to initiate outside intervention. This provides checks and balances in the intervention decision process and minimizes the likelihood of the responsibility felt by individual volunteers for what are often very hard decisions.

Our volunteers are trained in crisis intervention and suicide prevention skills. They also are trained to use our lethality scale and to know at what point that scale may indicate that outside intervention is needed. When I begin to see that I am dealing with a high level of lethality, I will let my on-call staff person know that I have a possible suicide in progress and that some intervention beyond what I can provide on the telephone may be needed. I would then be open to direction from the staff person. Our training program teaches volunteers how and when to use this consulting procedure and instills its value in us. The staff person is often consulted through a fellow-volunteer, and together they work out the logistics of checking past records, the criss-cross directory, calling the telephone company, and so on while I continue to work with the caller toward a positive resolution of the call. Such cooperative effort, often accomplished through the exchange of notes, enables the telephone intervention process to continue uninterrupted at the same time that steps are made to reach outside help if such should be needed as the call progresses or should it be terminated by the caller. If the call ends with a life-embracing decision by the caller, outside help can be quickly withdrawn.

Q: Most crisis lines cover a wide variety of problems, not just suicide. Suicide calls typically represent a small percentage of calls received; thus, only a small proportion of training time may be given to this area of service. What is your opinion about segregating a suicide hotline from the crisis center so that people trained to work on that hotline receive specific training in that area rather than in a smorgasbord of problems?

A (Wells): I think it may not make good sense to have just a suicide prevention center. Even those suicide prevention centers that advertise themselves as just that receive the majority of their calls for problems other than suicidal crises. To be a specialist in crisis intervention requires learning how to do a suicide assessment. This assessment is an essential aspect of all crisis work.

It has been noted that one of the problems with having a suicide prevention center is that potential callers may believe that one has to be suicidal or to talk about suicide as an admission ticket to call. In contrast, we have domestic violence hotlines or child-abuse hotlines whose callers may be suicidal. Volunteers at these services must know how to assess suicide risk among callers to these programs. The AAS certifies a variety of crisis programs, all of which have a responsibility to train volunteers or staff in dealing with suicidal callers even if they may represent a small proportion of calls received.

Q: Regarding taping calls for weekly supervision meetings with clinical staff, do you use these tapes to train volunteers as well, and do you secure written permission from the caller when you tape?

A (Stelmachers): We do not tape telephone calls but use taped face-to-face interviews. For those, we secure the client's permission by a written agreement. We play these tapes to other staff, students, and volunteers for training and supervision purposes. Therefore, the written authorization needs to state the intended audience and potential use of the tape.

This case illustrates well what can happen when we do not know what really occurred between the caller and the counselor. Even if we interviewed the counselor, she could verbally report her observations and thoughts about what happened but exclude important interactions to the extent that they were outside her level of awareness. A verbatim transcript or a tape of the interaction allows one to really get at the process of the interaction without the interference of the counselor's defenses.

Q: I would like to know more about the mechanics of matching call report forms from a phone line with those of the police or coroner's office in the event of a suicidal death or when trying to ascertain if a particular call ended in a suicide.

A (Stelmachers): One needs to secure an ongoing collaboration with the local medical examiner. The patient's name and mode of death are typically considered public information and therefore can be shared with an outside agency. The medical examiner's list of all individuals whose death was ruled suicide can be compared with a list of a suicide prevention center's callers/clients. In this way, the center can always find out if and when one of its clients has commited suicide—at least within the jurisdiction of a particular medical examiner. With the permission of the next of kin, the medical examiner may be willing to share more detailed records about the deceased (although this more detailed information is usually considered confidential and not available to the public).

Q: I am interested in the debriefing process. Is debriefing mandatory for all staff of the center? If not, which staff should be included? Are there any written guidelines available that describe how this process might proceed?

A (Stelmachers): At our center, we review all suicides and life-threatening suicide attempts. Outside professionals are sometimes invited if they can provide information that could help us better understand the suicide. In-patient suicides are regularly reviewed by the psychiatry department's Behavioral Emergency Advisory Committee. This is done according to suicide prevention policies and procedures.

A (Wells): In our center there is a list of people *required* to be there and a list of those *invited* to attend. All counselors who had direct contact with the client-caller must attend. Others, such as the director of clinical services and others who, for example, have done psychological autopsies, may be invited to attend depending on the situation. It may also be that we want our attorney present, as Dr. Stelmachers noted, to provide a measure of extra protection. In New Hampshire, the quality assurance records of a mental health center are not protected from discovery, so to provide that extra protection, we may want our attorney present. On the other hand, we may invite others who were involved in the case, such as the survivors, the police, and others, but their presence clearly makes the process discoverable by a court of law.

Q: I think the key issue here has to be how competently the center is administered. As Dr. Wells enumerated, the various standards, the administration, the training, the general service delivery, and so on are the issues that are going to control how well your volunteers perform.

But when I put myself in the shoes of this counselor, dealing with a suicidal caller in the wee hours of the morning, not communicating well, feeling like I'm losing her in spite of my training, I do not know whether I would have invoked some external authority to intervene, to try to hospitalize her. This client had a number of relationships other than this brief one with the counselor that perhaps could have been used. Then again, her mother is relieved after her death, and perhaps her friends were suicidal as well.

A (Stelmachers): As I mentioned before, all seven counselors whom I consulted stated that they would have intervened. This may, of course, reflect the setting in which we operate: a public teaching hospital with mostly professional staff. Therefore, we may be more willing to intervene more frequently and more readily than community-based centers using volunteers. The one element in this case that increased the immediate suicide risk was the fact that the young girl made the call in the middle of the night from a hotel room. She is obviously away from home, all by herself, with no one available in her immediate environment to intervene. There is little control over what she does in this situation. All staff members I talked to, individually and independently, would have intervened by either tracing the call or sending the police or ambulance.

A (Smith): I indicated in the questions I proposed that I think the counselor missed a number of areas of information that, had they been explored, might have led to an assessment of this case as a high-lethality suicide call. I do not know that the suicide would not have happened anyway, but the counselor would have had a different assessment of the call itself and might well have made a decision to initiate outside intervention procedures, which could have made a significant difference in the outcome of the call.

Audience comment: Our center cannot afford to provide supervisory staff to be available for all decision-making and outreach actions, so our volunteers progress with experience and training to that level. I believe that is an appropriate and good thing. A tragedy such as this case presents also is an opportunity. It forces the center and its personnel to evaluate themselves according to the very questions you are raising. Such an evaluation might affirm that the center is doing its job well. It might point to areas in need of change and improvement, a periodic process all centers should experience. Dr. Wells mentioned in his comments something I was told years ago, that if some of your callers don't kill themselves, you are probably not reaching your target population. That has helped our center through some difficult crisis situations.

Q: How might crisis centers contract with rescue services?

A (Wells): Crisis centers can contract with emergency services in the community to do outreach for them. It may be a two-way contract, with the emergency service contracting with the hotline to take their phone calls. The center, for example, could contract for outreach services or with a hospital for walk-in services.

Q: This case brings up the distinction between crisis intervention and counseling. These are two different methodologies and need to be clarified. How we conceptualize has much to do with how we practice.

A (Stelmachers): Both crisis intervention and counseling are needed. Although different in concept and practice, both approaches may need to be applied, sometimes consecutively, sometimes simultaneously.

Q: What impact would diagnostic information have had in the management of this case? What difference would it have made if we knew this patient was depressed or had a borderline personality disorder?

A (Stelmachers): It is my opinion that diagnoses are not sufficiently emphasized in programs that focus their training on supportive listening. I don't think we need to train volunteers to make DSM-III diagnoses, but clinical assessment of the mental status of the individual is invaluable for estimating suicide potential. Especially because mental illness has such a strong relationship to suicide, it would seem very important to have some diagnostic appreciation of whether an individual is manic, schizophrenic, psychotically depressed, a borderline personality, and so on. Suicide rates are known to be different for these various diagnostic categories, and the diagnostic differences make a much more significant contribution to suicide risk assessment than such demographic characteristics as sex, age, and similar items frequently found in suicide potential rating scales.

Q: Would you train volunteers to intervene differently based on that clinical assessment?

A (Stelmachers): Yes. The presence of absence of mental illness may dictate a different intervention strategy. Supportive listening, for instance, may not be sufficient if one is dealing with an individual who is currently psychotic. Because psychiatric patients are very much at risk for suicide, one needs to understand them, be able to diagnose them, and have the capacity to intervene in clinically appropriate ways. Without putting down the value of listening—which everybody seems to endorse as valuable—for the sickest population contacting suicide prevention centers, one needs the competence and capability to perform diagnostic evaluations, as well as administer treatment and emergency interventions.

REFERENCES

Action for mental health: Report of the Joint Commission on Mental Illness and Health. (1961). New York: Basic Books.

Litman, R. E. (1982). Hospital suicides: Lawsuits and standards. *Suicide and Life-Threatening Behavior, 12,* 212–220.

Shaffer, D., Garland, M. A., Gould, M., Fisher, P., & Trautman, P. (1988). Preventing teenage suicide. A critical review. *Journal of the American Academy of Child and Adolescent Psychiatry, 27,* 675–687.

Wells, J.O., & Hoff, L. A. (Eds.). (1984). *Certification standards manual for crisis intervention programs* (3rd ed.). Denver: American Association of Suicidiology. (Available from the AAS at 2459 So. Ash, Denver, CO 80222.)

References

II

Suicide Prevention in Clinical Practice

4

Issues in Therapy and Clinical Management: I

Models of secondary prevention stress early intervention and treatment, that is, the appropriate assessment of a patient as potentially suicidal and the offer and acceptance of a therapeutic intervention to improve the patient's level of functioning and decrease the risk for suicide. The patient's acceptance of an offer to help (compliance) is but one early ingredient in a complex recipe of factors related to the ultimate effectiveness of treatment. Other factors, such as the chronicity and severity of the patient's underlying pathology, the quality of alliance formed between patient and therapist, and the skill of the therapist, combine and interact to determine the success of any therapeutic intervention.

Overall, the effectiveness of current treatment programs (in particular for youth) has been evaluated by suicidologists as rather low (Eddy, Wolpert, & Rosenberg, 1987). Undoubtedly, this evaluation is based on a complex interplay of observations by these experts, relating to the level of training given professionals who ultimately must treat suicidal patients, to the consequent low level of quality in care generally provided these patients and to an admitted difficulty in working with difficult patients.

Clinicians know well enough that the ongoing treatment of a suicidal patient is an intricate and demanding process, involving often coexisting levels of treatment such as crisis intervention and long-term therapy; an anxiety-provoking experience, involving frequent and intense demands and emotionality, the ever-present threat of suicide or parasuicidal behavior, and fears of an ultimate suicidal death with its consequent malpractice suit (which, of course, will be lost as well); and one laden with a myriad of countertransferential feelings, which complicate an already complicated task (cf., Maltsberger, 1986). The process of therapy with a suicidal patient, simply put, is not an easy one.

With perhaps only slight hyperbole, it has been suggested that mental health professionals may be divided into two groups: those who have had a patient complete suicide and those who will. To the naive observer it may be tempting to construe a suicidal death of a therapy patient, ipso facto, as evidence of a treatment failure. It is common, as well, for therapists to respond to such experiences with feelings of responsibility, blame, and inadequacy (Goldstein & Buongiorno, 1984; Litman, 1965). Thus, therapists appear to believe that one's adequacy as a therapist may be judged according to having successfully avoided what is considered by the profession to be almost a sure bet!

Consider just one common type of suicidal patient, the borderline. The diagnosis of borderline personality disorder includes characteristics of impulsivity (often involving substance abuse), heightened affectivity, disturbed close relationships, an intolerance of being alone, low achievement in spite of apparent talent, mild psychotic experiences, and suicide attempts. Put more succinctly, the borderline personality is unstable and unpredictable.

Concurrently, many patients meeting criteria for a diagnosis of borderline personality disorder also present with sufficient critieria for a mood disorder. There is some debate in the literature regarding which diagnosis is primary: whether the depression is in response to the borderline patient's experience of aloneness, failures in relationships, and feelings of abandonment and badness or that these are outcomes of a depression leading to a definition of character (Gunderson, 1984). Irrespective of etiology, however, there is general agreement that suicidal behavior is a prominent feature of this disorder, the risk increasing when co-morbidity (with depression) is present (Friedman, Aranoff, Clarkin, Corn, & Hurt, 1983; McGlashan, 1987; Stone, Stone, & Hurt, 1987).

It is important to note that manipulative suicidal gestures and self-mutilative behaviors are common to this disorder but that completed suicides do occur. Estimates of completed suicides occurring within 5 years of hospital discharge range from 4.5% (Stone, 1982) to 7.6% (Stone et al., 1987). Among possible discriminating risk factors for these more lethal patients are affective co-morbidity and more frequent and extensive prior suicidal behavior (Kullgren, 1988). Preliminary data from another recent study of 40 female borderline inpatients (Shearer, Peters, Quaytman, & Wadman, 1988) suggest that advancing age, numerous previous suicide attempts, a history of psychotic manifestations and a family history of affective or substance abuse disorders may constitute a tentative risk profile for the more serious of attempters.

As noted, suicide gestures and attempts in this population are often referred to as manipulative, and indeed they often occur in an intense and unstable interpersonal context, typically one involving caregivers. Rage, vengeance, and an appeal for attention may motivate these behaviors more than does hopelessness and may stimulate in the therapist a range of "complementary identifications" (Kernberg, 1987) that can inhibit and paralyze the therapist, thus the therapy as well. Stone (1980) has described the process of work with the suicidal patient as follows: "The therapist and patient are locked into a game—for high stakes—which the therapist *must* win" (p. 65).

It is in this context that the following two cases regarding the clinical management of the suicidal patient are presented. The first case presents macrotherapeutic issues in the long-term treatment of the chronically suicidal, borderline patient. The second case focuses on a micro-therapeutic interaction. Both cases speak to the intensity and the intricacy of the therapeutic "game" with characterologically difficult patients, reflecting at once a myriad of questions of therapeutic style within a dynamic frame of ethics and legality.

Questions regarding the efficacy of treatment of the suicidal patient ultimately will be answered by the effectiveness with which clinicians master the complexities of these interactions. New models of old treatments (cf., Silver, Cardish, & Glassman, 1987) and of newer treatments (cf., Linehan, 1987) as well may make this task easier to accomplish in future years.

CASE STUDY: A SUICIDE PACT

Two women in their mid-30s were being seen by two different therapists. Patient A was treated by Therapist B and Patient C by Therapist D, each in psychoanalytically oriented psychotherapy once or twice weekly.

Patient A was a woman who had been divorced and remarried and had two small children. She had a history of repeated serious suicide attempts. Her current marriage was a very stormy one, and she had been involved in a number of extramarital relationships. When matters with her husband or lovers took a turn for the worse, she would make frighteningly serious suicide attempts, for example, soaking cotton balls with chloroform or carbon tetrachloride and putting them in a plastic bag that she would place over her head. She would also take massive overdoses of barbiturates, which she would obtain from various doctors. She would be admitted to the hospital in a serious condition, looking near death's door, would receive heroic medical treatment, and in a day or so would bounce back looking as fresh as a rose, charming both the nursing staff and other patients in the private psychiatric hospital, which Dr. B had admitted her to, with tales of her exploits.

Patient C was a divorced woman with no children who had a severe sciatic nerve injury secondary to an injection of phenothiazines that she had received when she was under the care of Therapist E. She harbored enormous rage toward Therapist E and intended to act out destructively toward him.

Patients A and C met each other when they were both hospitalized following suicide attempts, and they became fast friends. Ultimately, they entered into a suicide pact that Therapists B and D became aware of. Therapist B was inclined to hospitalize his patient whenever she appeared out of control; he had told her that if she felt that she was about to do something harmful to herself, he would prefer to admit her to the hospital briefly until she regained control. Therapist D, however, was inclined to a more laissez-faire attitude. He told Patient C that if she wanted to kill herself, he couldn't control that; further, that he couldn't work with her in therapy if she used suicide threats to manipulate him. Consequently, he refused to admit her unless she made some very serious attempt and he had no choice.

At one point Patients A and C decided to seek revenge on Therapist E by going to Therapist E's home and hiding themselves in a large child's dollhouse in the yard. They planned to kill themselves there so that Therapist E's 10-year-old daughter would discover them dead in the morning when she went out to play. They did go to the dollhouse on a Saturday evening, and each drank a fifth of vodka in order to kill herself, but they only passed out. They left in the morning, fortunately, before the child could discover them. Therapists B and D were told of this after the fact.

After approximately 3 years of intermittent inpatient and outpatient therapy requiring many hospitalizations—for some of which Therapist B had arranged to send Patient A to a state, rather than a private, hospital (Patient A received much secondary gain by "holding court" in the luxury of the private hospital in contrast to negative reinforcement in the more "therapeutic" but dungeon-like atmosphere of the state hospital)—Therapist B discovered that Patient A had been seeing another therapist for some 6 months during the same time that she was seeing him. He told her he would not treat her under those conditions and that she had to decide which therapist she wanted. She elected to go to the new therapist, and Therapist B lost contact with her. He learned some 6 months later that she killed herself.

Patient C continued with Therapist D for about 1 year after Patient A had died; then she too killed herself.

The presenting issue relates to the management of the suicidal patient and the contrast between a laissez-faire and a more paternalistic and controlling therapeutic style.

COMMENTARY

Andrew Slaby:

Clinical decisions regarding chronically suicidal patients are never easy. Sometimes, however, they are more difficult than at other times. This is particularly true when more than one therapist is involved. This situation occurs when various family members are seen by different therapists, when a patient is simultaneously in couples or family therapy and individual therapy, when a patient is receiving medication from a psychopharmacologist and verbal therapy from a psychotherapist and, as in the instance of this case study, when two members of a suicide pact are seeing different therapists.

Biological, psychological, social, and existential factors must be considered in the evaluation and management of any self-inflicted destructive behavior. These clinical variables are considered in the context of extant legal restraints in determining a course of therapeutic action.

Excellent medical care and exacting legal action do not by definition, alone or together, define the most ethical or humane approach. What may be good for an individual at one time may not be at another time. Nor is what is good for one person necessarily good for another in the same circumstances but with a different background. At times permissiveness allows enhancement of patients' self-esteem by allowing them to personally master a problem. This is, in fact, how children who may be at the same developmental level as some severely characterologically disturbed adult patients acquire an internalized sense of control and therefore good self-esteem. At other times, however, failure to provide criteria whereby a person can quantify success at attainment of certain developmental goals suggests to patients, as it does to children, that the therapist (or parent in the case of children) does not care. The impression is that the therapist (or parent) does not sufficiently value the patient (or child) to establish guidelines for behavior or that the therapist, like a mother or father who had difficulty parenting, cannot endure the anger created by boundary setting that allows growth.

Issues raised in this particular case are the relative benefits of a laissez-faire and a paternalistic policy in managing suicidal behavior, the best approach to termination of a therapeutic relationship, and the need for limit setting in treatment. Each issue has clinical, legal, and ethical dimensions.

Clinically, when psychiatric illness occurs, perception of patients' reality is distorted. This impairment of perception dictates a need to set limits for these patients, much as perceptual lag in a child's development necessitates parental guidelines or supervision.

Mood disorders and schizophrenia, like medical illnesses such as Alzheimer's disease and toxic psychoses, compromise reality testing. Major depression and bipolar (manic-depressive) disorders are real illnesses that, in a manner similar to an organic brain syndrome, affect the perception of reality of those suffering from them. Profoundly depressed people cannot make an informed choice any more than can a person with prednisone- or beta-blocker-induced depression. For example, a brilliant young internist was jubilant after being granted a position in an Ivy League medical school. He had a loving wife and three beautiful children and had always wanted to be a professor of medicine. Something happened, however. Over 4 weeks in June, he spoke of his wife as being vapid; his children bored him; he told his colleagues that he was a lousy physician and that he had never wanted to be a doctor. One day he didn't come to the hospital. He was found hanging in his basement. He had told his wife he was depressed, but she saw no need to "force" him to seek the psychiatric help he needed but felt too busy to spare the time for. Six weeks before his death he commenced and continued until his death the use of the antihypertensive medication reserpine for high blood pressure first diagnosed in medical school. Reserpine was initiated after several other antihypertensives had failed to regulate his condition. Reserpine causes depletion of catecholamine in the brain resembling the relative deficit seen with major depression. "Why," his colleagues queried, "didn't he cease use of a drug that all medical students know causes depression as a side effect?" Because of his severe depression, he viewed the world through blue-tinted glasses. He did not see himself as "ill" and therefore treatable. He considered himself "worthless," "helpless," and most malignantly, "hopeless."

There are a number of other instances in which self-destructive behavior may be manifested without a DSM-III-R mood disorder. These include the majority of depressions that attend cases of substance abuse, terminal illness, and extreme social circumstances. In the first instance, an individual feels hopelessness in his or her attempt to desist from alcohol, crack, or other substance use. This may lead to suicide. If the individual is detoxified and remains alcohol and drug-free, the depression lifts in the majority of cases (Gold & Slaby, in press). Both cancer and AIDS are associated with increased risk of suicide (Slaby, 1989). In both instances, as the illnesses progress, patients become despairing of cure. Similarly, people who feel entrapped in abusive marriages for economic, social, or child-rearing reasons may feel the only reprieve will be death— natural or self-inflicted. The majority of suicides, however, are associated with a treatable mood disorder. There is hope, and this hope has a relatively fixed time frame. On the whole, depressed individuals respond to medication, but it takes 3 weeks to 3 months to achieve therapeutic serum levels and to be fully relieved of depression. For this reason we see increased risk of suicide with psychopharmacologic treatment; that is, energy returns before the distortions of perception are alleviated, resulting in self-destruction (Slaby, 1986).

In the patient being discussed (Patient A), the diagnosis is unclear. Dysthymic disorder and narcissistic and borderline personality disorders are considerations. Treated or untreated, this patient might have repeated suicide attempts. The relative efficacy of hospitalization in treatment of such a patient is a point of controversy. Some argue for protection of a person from death or self-inflicted disability and monitored clinical trials with medications such as antidepressants or mood stabilizing drugs, including anticonvulsants such as carbamazapine and valproate, which impact on impulsivity. Others feel that hospitalization reinforces acting out of self-destructive behavior and that drugs make some of these patients feel worse, enhancing the desire to die or hurt oneself to "feel more real." Brief hospitalization and/or intense outpatient treatment in selected cases allows bonding with a therapist, which may serve to modify intensity of pain and therefore be prophylactic against self-destructive behavior. This may also enhance compliance with therapeutic trials of monamine oxidase inhibitors and other mood-stabilizing agents, which cannot be cavalierly administered to patients who abuse drugs with self-destructive intent.

Legally, the central issue is the degree to which a person must be destructive to self or others to require involuntary confinement. Some therapists will not consider hospitalization unless an actual attempt has been made or is imminent. Generally, the legal counsel of a hospital advises clinicians to provide the best clinical care and leave the legal consequences to them. It is better to defend a clinician who achieves the highest standard of care than it is to defend one who compromises care and loses a patient to death although appearing on paper to be legally correct. Ethical resolution is somewhere between the extreme letter of the law and a scientific imperative. In that gray zone lies the person, the person's civil rights, and the person's right to receive good care.

In most states, patients cannot be hospitalized against their will unless they have a *mental illness and are an immediate danger to themselves or others.* It is clear that if suicidal behavior is a product of real mental illness, a clinician must hospitalize patients to protect them, just as one must prevent patients intoxicated with alcohol from driving to protect the patients themselves and others. Patients without DSM-III-R illness can be considered dangerous to themselves if, for example, they have AIDS, amyotrophic lateral sclerosis (Lou Gehrig's disease), or Huntington's chorea without dementia or depression and decide they would rather die than suffer the expected progression of the disease.

Despite the absence of a treatable mental illness, a clinician or hospital may be found remiss if, following diagnosis or worsening of a terminal or painfull ilness, a person commits or attempts suicide or attempts and is left mutilated. The usual approach today is either to seek counsel for the ethics committee of a hospital or from the hospital's legal counsel. Prevention of suicide can usually be achieved within a hospital, but upon discharge the patient will have, for better or worse, the freedom of choice to make the decision regarding to what degree compromise of quality of life can be tolerated and to what degree the expected negative effects of suicide on those who survive is less tolerable than the psychic pain they suffer. Families of patients with deteriorating and/or extremely painful or limiting illness should be made aware that suicide may be an option elected.

In the absence of mental disorder and immediate danger to self or others, involuntary hospitalization is without cause. Some people, such as substance abusers, may change rapidly and kill themselves in a toxic state. Without a *recent* history of repeated drug use with repeated attempts, this, unfortunately, cannot usually be predicted. Without warning and obvious immediate risk factors, a clinician cannot be held accountable for such suicides.

Finally, there are mental disorders that lack available treatment that could successfully reduce suicide risk. In other cases, all known approaches to management have failed. Some hospitals are hesitant to admit borderline patients because attending physicians do not feel hospitalization holds promise for significant impact. Those at this extreme feel that the usual course of a borderline patient is impulsive behavior with or without suicide attempts until, with time, such a patient matures, burns out, or dies. A common course is repeated suicide attempts in the younger years, with chronic depression and anger more predominant in later years. With major depression, suicide attempts more frequently result in death.

Ethical concerns regarding the right to die by suicide involve the impact on the patients themselves, on their families, and on society. An individual may feel alone and without responsibility to family or society, but if an attempt fails and that person is left paralyzed or brain-damaged, the cost to society is significant. Limited health care resources are deployed, but these are ambivalently received if patients maintain awareness of their situation or may be unappreciated despite the cost to society and others in need. An individual may feel hopelessly depressed and refractory to treatment by the most distinguished clinicians; but if the patient dies, the survivors are passively but irrevocably affected. Just as a survivor who lost someone dear in the Holocaust never forgets and finds the horror of that reality a subterranean existential theme in all they do, so too, someone who has lost a loved one to suicide *never* forgets. Survivors can learn to undersand, but they cannot forget. The increased risk of suicide when an individual has lost a family member to suicide probably not only relates to both biogenetic and psychodynamic factors but also to the ever-present reality that human love and relationship were not perceived by the deceased as sufficient to deter self-inflected death. A suicide attempt in the next generation may be as much an existential debt being paid in kind and suffered in communion as is survivor guilt in the Holocaust. Joy is forever compromised. A part of the self is already dead and beckons to that part still alive to join in death to complete the tragic reality. In a similar vein, there is the risk of the greater community seen with suicide epidemics. These imitative suicides that sometimes cluster are an unintended consequence to society.

Self-inflicted death has from time immemorial invited and excited response. To some degree an underlying issue in so-called rational suicide, in the absence of affective or other major organic mental illness, concerns who ultimately is to decide the individual's fate: the individual or society. If it is the individual, then obviously suicide is an option that may be exercised. If it is society, then suicide may be legally banned. Despite the latter, in some subcultures the individual may be presented with the option of suicide. St. Augustine cautioned early Christians against public proclamation of their newly embraced faith for fear the new religion would be without a body of the faithful to minister to those in need and proselytize the good news. It was a commonly held belief that baptism by blood through martyrdom promised immediate entry into Paradise. It also resulted in considerable loss of life that would have been prevented if the overly zealous had not openly invited death from nonbelieving Romans. Was this suicide or religious fervor?

Comparably, kamikaze pilots in World War II were doomed to death but were seen as heroes rather than failed men to be disgraced. Jews elected to die by their own hand when their fort was under siege at Masada, rather than be killed by the Romans. Many Jews and non-Jews alike elected suicide in Nazi Germany rather than be subject to denigration, torture, and death in concentration camps.

How does the decision to die by suicide, rather than suffer progressive dementia or painful or functional and physical deterioration by diseases such as multiple sclerosis, AIDS, and cancer, differ from some of these historical precedents? These are not easy questions to answer. Nor, for that matter, are they easy questions to ask. One thing is certain. Suicides by people with DSM-III-R disorders are for the most part preventable, given available treatments. Even untreated, a number of these patients will experience remission with time if they do not suicide, although the course until remission may be painful to family, patient, and therapist alike. The distortion of perception makes one feel hopeless. In many cases, such people have not been sufficiently evaluated to determine to what degree treatable biologic illness is present. Subsequently, they have not received diagnostic-specific therapeutic interventions. Ethical considerations in care relate to providing alternatives for care when that provided by a clinician has failed in part or completely.

Existential psychoanalytic or cognitive therapy approaches may succeed where psychoanalytic therapy has reached a stalemate. There are many classes of antidepressants, mood-stabilizing agents, and other biological approaches, including electroconvulsive therapy (ECT) that have caused the sun to rise for those who felt damned to an endless night of despair. Victor Frankl encourages us to help patients find a "why" to live so that they find a "how" to live. Others speak of teaching patients to change what they can in their lives to better tolerate what they cannot change. This is summed up in the Tranquility Prayer of Alcoholics Anonymous and is a form of cognitive therapy. Monoamine oxidase inhibitors alone or in conjunction with tricyclic antidepressants may ameliorate depression when the latter alone fails. Lithium, carbamazapine, valproate, and thyroid supplementation all have been used to augment the effect of antidepressant therapy. Sociotherapy to develop a psychological family when a biological one is either psychologically or physically absent is another approach sometimes neglected by those of a more individual dyadic therapeutic bent.

Exploring how pleasure, joy, humor, or religion, alone or in combination, may be found to temper existential angst or severe weltsmertz is another approach. A medieval mystic, when asked "Is life worth living?" responded: "If one need ask the question, it is possible that one has not lived, and most certain that one has not loved." Life may be "tsuras" or a "vale of tears" for many, but human love does, despite all, periodically allow moments of unexpected joy to emerge.

In this particular case I would prefer not to be either Patient A or C or Therapist B, D, or E. Unfortunately, we often have no choice. I myself tend to be conservative and to hospitalize if a patient is acutely suicidal. Death or mutilation is irrevocable, whereas hospitalization allows a patient to leave the hospital at some point, alive and intact. If there is no immediate danger to self, there is really little choice if the patient refuses to be hospitalized. Borderline patients cannot be hospitalized each and every time they think of wanting to kill themselves.

There are so many different psychological and biological approaches that need to be exhausted before a case can be truly labeled refractory. Different therapists impact in different ways at different times. Therapies and therapists may act additively or synergistically. In this instance, monamine oxidase inhibitors, existential psychoanalytic approaches, enhancement of social supports and self-esteem, and active work to integrate the patient with self-help, religious, and community groups may favorably complement the work of the most seasoned therapists.

Therapists' hope and optimism may have a momentary impact. Conversely, difficult and recurrently life-threatening patients frustrate therapists. Frustration leads to anger. Therapists' anger is contagious, potentially leading to acting out by both patients and therapists. I would be aware that my own frustration at seeing a patient not respond could lead not only to anger but to a sense of hopelessness in myself that might be sensed by a patient. These countertransference issues have been discussed in depth by others (Maltsberger & Buie, 1974). Patients can pick up a therapist's anger or sense of hopelessness and suicide. At such times it may be best to seek consultation or get another therapist involved in the treatment.

From a legal perspective, the therapist-patient relationship can be terminated if a patient is sufficiently forewarned and if other options, particularly that of transfer to another therapist, are provided the patient pursuant to the final session. Hospitalization may result from the termination. If so, transfer to the new therapist should occur at the time of the hospitalization.

Rules in treatment vary but are necessary for protection of patients and therapists. Different therapists have different approaches, which may be effective at different times in the course of therapy. It is advisable for a therapist to forewarn a patient that if repeated suicide attempts do not diminish, another therapist may be appropriate to obtain a stabilizing impact on behavior. One person cannot be totally responsible 24 hours a day, 7 days a week, for the care of extremely suicidal patients. Multiple therapists, providing evening and weekend coverage, reduce burnout and allow a more sustained enthusiasm in therapy than is possible if one therapist is continually responsible for patients as suicidal as the women in this case. I believe that *if* I were the ideal therapist for this patient, there would be a diminishing number of telephone calls and suicide attempts. Obviously, no "ideal" therapist exists.

Sometimes, also, patients are intractably, chronically ill. As a last resort, these patients are often referred to the most skilled therapists; yet they exhaust, test, and frustrate the most sophisticated psychodynamic, social, existential, and biologic intervention, "burning out" very good therapists. Concurrent consultation or supervision may not only enhance quality of care but also reduce burnout. Again, transfer to another therapist may be required.

A prominent surgeon once looked up at me as he closed a wound at an operation at which I assisted and said, "Man proposes; God disposes." What he meant was that no matter how skilled a surgeon is (and he was one of the best), he or she does not heal a wound. Excellent surgeons only set the circumstances for wound healing. The rest is left to nature or God. Therapists are many times in a position in which they are made to feel—by patients, their families, society, or often themselves—that they should be able to cure everyone. The most skilled cardiologists should have higher mortality rates in their patient population than do those less skilled if indeed they are referred the sickest in last resort. Those who are the most suicidal should seek help from those who have the greatest experience in successfully managing such patients.

In most instances, those with the greatest expertise bring a unique approach to a problem. This results in either rapid resolution or longevity that would not be possible without seeking such consultation. In other instances, as in the case of patients with severe cardiac disease, who may be beyond any human intervention and who die despite consultation from the most eminent cardiologist, therapists who accept the most severely suicidal patients will at times experience loss of a patient by suicide. Such therapists may have a greater knowledge of management of the chronically suicidal, despite their greater mortality rate. We should always applaud their courage, their hope, and their personal sacrifice in trying to manage the vicissitudes of the human experience at a level at which they, no more than their patients, cannot deny the limitations of the human form.

Kim Smith:

The case description provides little information on which the psychoanalytically oriented clinician could specifically focus. Limited to what the patients and therapist did to each other, the description encourages focusing on behavioral interventions. Suicidal behavior is a symptom that has many possible etiologies, motivations, and meaning, depending on a person's psychology. To precisely understand these two women, then, requires our knowing how their therapists understood their drives, the maturity of their consciences, their relative abilities to maintain an observing posture with regard to their thoughts and actions, and their capacities to retain adequate judgment and reality testing in the face of emotional turmoil.

Psychoanalytic treatment has alternative treatment approaches; the selection of a particular approach is based on an evaluation of factors such as those just mentioned. In order to apply an analytic perspective to this material, it is necessary for me to be arbitrary and speculative in my evaluation of the cues provided.

Patient A

I believe that Patient A may be productively understood as a narcissistic character organized within the upper borderline range of ego functioning. Clearly, her action orientation (i.e., two stormy marriages, several affairs, several hospitalizations) could reflect more serious borderline functioning. However, there are also cues suggesting that her action tendency may be part of a higher-functioning ego. Specifically, her hospital stays were apparently not characterized by the chaotic, hostilely challenging, or angrily withdrawing behaviors of the borderline patient. Instead, she repeatedly set up a positvely controlling role, what the therapist referred to as "holding court," which, although not therapeutic, appears reflective of more stable objective relations tendencies. Also, consider the fact that she saw a second therapist for a full 6 months before it became evident to Therapist B. Being willing to conceal this fact for so long suggests that the patient did not rely on defensive splitting, such as would have been suggested if she had actively exploited the differences between the therapists. A lower-level borderline patient would have poor frustration tolerance and a decided preference for indulging in excitedly chaotic interactions (Masterson, 1976) and therefore would not likely have passed up such an opportunity. I would be more inclined to think of an even higher level of functioning, such as found in the hysterical character, if it were not for her willingness to join with Patient C in acting so sadistically toward Patient C's ex-therapist. The fact that she permitted herself participation at all is incongruent with the typical demand of the hysterical patient's conscience for conventionality and high moral ground.

For the purpose of our current discussion, I will assume that Patient A's narcissistic character and ready sense of insult from others shaped her suicide dynamics. Specifically, it likely created a feeling of being helpless to otherwise exercise control over the perceived neglect, deprivation, or humiliation from others. Her seriously determined suicidal actions, then, were aimed at restoring control over valued others: if death did occur, then so be it—the others would have their lives spoiled and would forever hurt for their wrongs. Her suicidal actions revealed her determination not to relinquish tight control over sources of narcissistic nurturance (i.e., "part objects"). Under these circumstances the therapist's preemptive hospitalizations underscored the seriousness of her complaints to the "depriving" other. Whether the "depriving other" was the loved one or the therapist, he or she likely felt pressured into being more giving and responsive to her. She likely felt elated and back in control at such times, whereas others very probably felt furious. The therapist may well have been angrily acting in response to his personal sense of impotence to make an impact on her by having her hospitalized at the state hospital. If he believed that the "dungeon-like atmosphere of the state hospital" was truly best for her, then why did he not consistently hospitalize her there?

Given these perspectives, how might we approach the treatment of Patient A? An initial diagnostic process would have generally informed us about her narcissistic dynamics and have revealed her various ego strengths and ego weaknesses. A good example of how to conduct such diagnostic work can be found in Kernberg's (1984) outline of the "structural interview." If it were apparent, for instance, that when attempting to control others she retained her abilities to use good judgment, to remain reality-anchored, and to observe herself, then her treatment in outpatient psychotherapy was appropriate. I will assume that this was true and that she could have been treated in an outpatient therapy. That therapy should have been frequent (at least twice a week) in order to help her make an emotional investment in her therapist. When working with narcissistic patients, especially ones that are fairly detached, the therapist needs to be an important presence in their lives. Initially, the therapist can help that occur with structure: meeting frequently with the patient. After an attachment forms, as well as the various kinds of transferences that narcissistic patients begin to develop, the therapist can cut back to once a week or so (if finances warrant). Without such an investment, the relationship issues that prompted her acting out would have been too vague and uncompellingly developed within the therapy to be interpreted. Patients who feel an excessive need for control must be helped to anticipate their behaviors. The therapist cannot be unresponsive to the suicidal crises of the patient with significant ego weakness and must be ready to intervene and hospitalize if necessary. This is especially true for the patient with narcissistic deficits. Not actively responding can further reinforce the narcissistic character's internalized images of parents who could not accurately hear what their child needed nor trouble themselves to respond.

Patient C

Patient C appears to have more significant ego weakness than Patient A and therefore required a more structured and supportive therapeutic approach. Patient C's anger appears more primitive and consciously sadistic in nature, as indicated in her formulation of the plan for revenge on her previous therapist. This level of sadism speaks to her capacity to consciously accept relatively unneutralized aggressive impulses such as are often seen in lower borderline and psychotic patients. I believe Patient C was in the lower borderline range. In appraising her level of ego functioning, we can also consider the fact that she was administered phenothiazine IM, a type of major tranquilizer that is given by injection primarily when a patient becomes uncontrollably psychotic or angry. The fact of this injection, then, provides further suggestion of this patient's weakened ego structures.

The suicide pact suggests that both patients had a commitment to a destructive course of acting out. A suicide pact is a commitment to destruction and should be very vigorously confronted by the therapists. The therapist, apparently recognizing the patient's acceptance of angry acting out as a manipulative tool, attempted to set clear limits around their work, reminding her of her responsibility to stay alive and of the antitherapeutic impact of her manipulation. This tack, although defensible with higher-functioning patients, is usually ineffective with lower borderline or psychotic patients. The strong feelings these patients have produce shifting senses of their evaluations of themselves and of others (i.e., shifting ego states). Commitments to think before acting that are made in one ego state can seem distant and unreasonable when the patient is feeling furious or humiliated. Being cognizant of such instability, the therapist needs to be very active and involved with any such patient he or she agrees to treat. The lower borderline patient will project rage, revenge, and sadistic ideas onto the therapist who often must simply contain them while persistently working to stimulate ego structures to work more effectively, tolerate less splitting, neutralize aggressive internal images by aiding in the internalizing of the therapist's more mature responses, and help the patient to appreciate the cost of such impulsive acting out. Hospitalization is often required for this process. If the patient is without resources to pay for hospitalization and yet has such a weakened ego that even a very supportive outpatient treatment cannot be effective, then the therapist should not attempt treatment with psychotherapy. Instead, medication and crisis intervention treatment are called for. We should not extend ourselves to treat patients we do not believe we can treat, that is, those lacking the ego or other resources to benefit.

We can make use of therapist's heightened concern for manipulation to develop a point about overly rule-conscious clinicians. Too much attention to rules and structures can be defenses used by a therapist to avoid feeling vulnerable or becoming aware of sexual or aggressive feelings for the patient. In this case, we wonder if Patient C's therapist was so guarded as to be constricted in his capacity to be empathically in tune with her. To the extent that this speculation is correct, we can go a step further and infer that an important dynamic for Patient C was her tendency to respond to perceived deprivation with attacking, revenge-driven anger. In reality, such anger usually stimulates others to withdraw or to act angrily and deprivingly via the process of projective identification.

General Technical Considerations

In the last paragraph of the clinical vignette, we were encouraged to connect the eventual suicide of each woman with the contrasting sytles of the therapists. Therapist B is labeled as "more paternalistic and controlling" and Therapist D is described as "laissez-faire." Obviously, such stylistic differences, if that is what they are, were both associated with negative outcomes.

The "styles" of Therapists B and D, however, have particular interest when they are considered as possible reflections of countertransference acting out. There are real differences in conceptualizing the therapist's response to the suicidal patient that are passionately argued in the literature. However, to discuss these differences productively requires many more details about the patients, about the fabric of therapy, and about the therapists and their conduct; with anything less, the debate becomes very abstract and polemic.

One technical question is whether the treatment experiences of either patient were "focused." When suicidal impulses become apparent, some modification in analytic process is usually found to be beneficial. Specifically, rather than continuing to encourage the patient's free-associative wandering over the internal landscape of his or her mind, the therapist needs to listen selectively for derivatives of the suicidal impulse, explore with the patient the function of these derivatives, and appropriately inquire about the patient's closeness to action. The suicidal impulse will be closely related to having to adjust or relinquish unrealistic hopes about core conflict issues. This selective, clarifying, interpretive concentration on the death impulses and their relationship to core conflicts is what is meant by a "focused therapy." Studies at the Menninger Foundation (Eyman, 1987) have shown that therapists with patients who have committed suicide often have considerable difficulty pursuing core conflict issues, especially when the patient hinted at becoming very angry or very depressed or threatened implicitly to leave the therapy.

Another technical question is whether the patient's psychotherapy sessions occurred with sufficient frequency. An indication that this may not have been the case is that the acting out was so poorly contained within the therapy hours. The absence of such containment usually indicates either that the type of therapy was inappropriate, given the patient's level of ego organization, or that the therapy was not occurring frequently enough for acting out to be absorbed in it. It should be a very significant concern, one worthy of consultation with a colleague, when the therapy does not follow the expected path, containing more and more of the patient's acting out over time. In regard to this and other issues, I wonder if these therapists made use of respected colleagues in a consultation or supervisory process.

My final comment is not based on the case material per se but rather on my experience with suicidal patients and as a supervisor of other therapists. It is impressive how many therapists, without significant reflection, respond to a suicidal patient's "hopelessness" by efforts to dispel it. Even in the clinical writings of respected colleagues (e.g., Shneidman, 1985) we are seldom encouraged to study the meaning of hopelessness for a given individual. Instead, some therapists retreat from important confrontation or interpretation when it is anticipated that the patient will feel hopeless. Perhaps this retreat happens because if the patient feels hopeless, the therapist will often feel impotent and unskilled. Thus, the retreat becomes a conclusive defense against both the patient's and the therapist's dwelling on unpleasant feeling associated with very devalued views of themselves. However, there is great value in attempting to learn what the patient is hopeless about and in narrowing this immobilizing affect so that it becomes a feeling about something specific. Some of the things that are hoped for may be truly without hope. Our patients need to feel hopeless about certain expectations of themselves and others when these expectations are unrealistic and need to be relinquished. As Erna Furman (1984) teaches us, psychological depression is an affect experienced when a person clings to an unreachable goal or object. One of the therapeutic tasks, then, is to help the patient transform depression into "sadness," the emotion experienced when a loss has been accepted. Until the loss has been accepted, patients are very apt to depressively grind away at their yearning for the impossible and depreciate the value of the possible.

In the last analysis, we must listen carefully to our patients, learn how to ask the necessary diagnostic questions, focus the therapy on the relationship between the suicidal impulse and the core conflicts, and help them to feel appropriately hopeless so that mourning and rebuilding can occur. The therapist who substitutes a rigid style or slavish adherence to technique for such efforts is apt to be a poor therapist for the suicidal patient.

Marc Hertzman:

This case vignette involves two similar and intertwined cases of serious, chronic suicidal behavior. My commentary highlights two issues that I consider to be central to the portrayal rendered here and a few others that might raise some questions for the reader.

The first concern has to do with the whole series of differentiations around what is ethical and what is legal, particularly in the practice of dealing with suicidal patients; the second is a caveat about the need to view each case individually and, in so doing, to think about options that might broaden the therapist's likelihood of being helpful, as well as the patient's choices.

As a hospital psychiatrist, when I walk down the street and happen to see patients from my inpatient service out of context there, taking a pass on the street, they seem quite unusual to me. However, when I walk down the hall in the hospital, they seem quite ordinary. After a while, you begin to accustom yourself to seeing people in a certain kind of way. It is helpful to stand back from routines and think about different and perhaps more useful ways of assessing people's problems.

When mental health professionals invoke the word *ethics*, they often mean it as pejorative of another professional's practices. To bastardize it, "What I do [with suicidal patients] is 'ethical' if it meets my standards." My understanding of what we at least *ought* to mean when we are talking about ethical issues is different from that. It is that an ethical issue is a question that usually does not have an easy and obvious answer. Ethics are codes or guides to behavior when issues pose at least two possible choices or decisions to be made. The course of action one takes depends on considerations such as one's personal values, the culture that one lives in, religious considerations, and the like. The study of ethics generally suggests that a knowledge of the underpinnings in values, morals, religion, and culture are often helpful in understanding the basis or rationale for decision making.

When we are talking about an approach to dealing with a patient who has a high-risk potential for suicide, as both of the patients presented here had most of the time, we are talking about the kinds of choices of stance that a therapist takes toward a patient. I consider that first and foremost an ethical question. What is essential about that is that one be as clear as one can about what is one's own basis for selecting alternatives, including background, upbringing, and one's own values and concerns. In turn, that presumably enables us to have a greater degree of respect for what another person's values may be. I belabor this because I think that, when it comes to issues dealing with patients who are acutely suicidal, ethical and legal considerations may be in conflict with one another at times.

In the present instance, at least two styles of approach to the management of the chronically suicidal patient emerge, and they are respectively labeled as "laissez-faire" and "more paternalistic and controlling." In practice, of course, such a contrast is likely to be incomplete and infinitely more complex. Nonetheless, as a matter of style in approach, it strikes me that the dichotomy proposed is probably a legitimate and real one in professional discourse on the subject and therefore worthy of elaboration.

The laissez-faire approach, in which the therapist concedes at the outset that he or she is powerless to prevent the patient's ultimate suicide, is often the approach romantically favored by mental health professionals. Perhaps this is because it is generally consistent with a "liberal" position on politics, civil rights, and the like. The stance probably must be that of the relatively disinterested consultant, whose task it is to stand ready and willing to help understand not only the patient's verbalizations, emotions, fantasies, and fears but also the patient's actions. The therapist draws limits around actually assisting by intervening when suicide is being threatened or when the patient is threatening dangerous actions.

What often makes the laissez-faire approach a compromise is the legal imperative. In many jurisdictions, the therapist (of whatever professional stripe) is subject to more specific directives, mostly implicit in court decisions, to protect life and limb above most other considerations. This involves not merely the duty to warn (*Tarasoff 1974/1976*), a fairly narrowly constructed obligation, but the broader one of reasonably trying to anticipate and doing everything possible to apprehend patients—and others, for that matter—before self-harm ensues. For example, in most jurisdictions this would now include attempting to hold the patient against his or her will if the therapist thinks that suicide is of substantial likelihood to occur within the near future. In a sense, this is the legal corner into which psychiatry has gradually helped government to paint psychiatrists and other mental health professionals, by claiming an expertise in prediction that may or may not really exist in fact.

The capacity for patients (not necessarily consciously motivated, to be sure) to maneuver therapists into the position of having to be dictatorial and controlling should never be underestimated. In the case vignette, this proved to be a problem for both therapists, notwithstanding their differences in philosophical conviction. The laissez-faire therapist was taking a much greater risk of liability in this regard. The point is not that a therapist should therefore demur from the laissez-faire position. Rather, it is that, in the best of all worlds, therapists should undertake this knowingly and with a willingness to suffer the consequences of being wrong in their estimates of any particular episode.

As a second point of emphasis, I would like to discuss the need to view each person individually and, in fact, each suicide attempt as a separate episode. Given the nature of this case conference, we could not reasonably have had access to all of the details of each case that would have helped us decide on the best course(s) of action. However, I would like to make a plea that, each time the issue of potential suicide arises, adequate inquiry into the details surrounding the threat take place. (Dr. Smith has gone into this point in great depth in his consultation.) Generalizations about what therapists should or should not do are good and useful as guides to actions. However, they can easily obscure particular possibilities that might be helpful in more limited ways.

It seems to me that at least two bits of data from the case presentation can be brought to bear on this point, the necessity of considering the particular in addition to the general. For one, both patients were treated throughout in "psychoanalytically oriented psychotherapy." This type of therapy has been and remains the predominant modus operandi among all disciplines doing psychotherapy in this country and is certainly well within accepted practice. However, one wonders whether the reader's response to this case vignette would have been the same had the description read instead, "cognitive-behavioral," "rational-emotive,"

"Jungian" therapy, or the like. We are all in some sense circumscribed by what we have learned and the climate in which we practice. Nonetheless, one wonders whether other alternatives to therapy in either of these cases would have been more productive.

In particular, Patient A was never noted to have any supporters with whom the therapist or other therapists worked during the course of her illness. Whether family therapy or couples therapy was indicated, because acting-out behavior was a primary mode of expression in therapy, it was inevitable that the therapist would have important and even urgent contacts with a number of other people in the patient's life to whom she was crucial. What was the impact of her suicide attempts on her children, both immediate and permanent? And what is the therapist's obligation to the next generation in this regard?

Also, the suicide compact occurred in the context of serious alcohol abuse by both patients, and the details became known to both therapists. Was this substance abuse, and should it have been treated as a separate, acute issue, not merely an outcome of character pathology or affective dysregulation? What about the compact? Given that both patients and both therapists were apprised of the facts, would some variety of face-to-face encounter—for example, conjoint treatment—have defused a potentially explosive dyad at a certain crisis point in treatment?

Finally, I should remark on the very process of case consultation. Consultation in the course of treatment of the sucidial patient is often helpful, especially, from a relatively disinterested point of view, to delineate countertransferential issues. I believe that it is precisely through such willingness to undergo self-examination that we shall most likely improve our ability to deal more effectively with such patients.

Questions and Responses

Comment (Slaby): As therapists, I think we don't discuss enough of what we are all aware of. There are times when our patients make us very angry, when they so frustrate us, intrude in our lives or create problems for us, that we feel enraged. I believe it is at these times that we may need to consider seeking consultation or supervision. In some instances, that patient may have to see someone else.

Even less frequently discussed is our empathy for our patients' hopelessness. Truly empathic therapists pick up the hopelessness of the patient and become like an echo chamber for the patient. I know two women who have AIDS, contracted from transfusion for breast surgery in one instance and for cancer of the colon in the other. They are hopeless. They feel life has been very unfair. If they talk about their hopelessness with someone who is very empathic, their felt despair may be reflected in the other person's eyes. It *is* unfair. It *is* hopeless. These women are not getting better. We forget sometimes that those of us who are the very best of therapists for many patients, because we ride every nuance of emotion like a ripple of water, may, because of this sensitivity, mirror back frustration and despair. This is both an irony and a great difficulty that therapists need to address.

Q: How would you deal with this woman now? How would you treat this hysterical, borderline patient differently from the way she was treated?

A (Hertzman): I think there are some things we may have under-emphasized in our discussion that may deal with this question. One of these has to do with the obvious substance abuse that occurred around the compact, which raises the question of how much more was going on in either patient and, in the face of that, whether a talking treatment of the type rendered can, in fact, proceed in any useful way.

There is one area where I suspect Dr. Smith and I are in disagreement or at least have a difference in emphasis. I think of all therapy as supportive. The only question is, what does it support? Particularly with borderline patients—especially low-functioning borderlines but, frankly, as far as I'm concerned, with *all* borderlines—I think the emphasis should be supportive, understanding that nothing is pure and that there are times when one can deal with issues that may, in fact, provoke strong emotional responses intentionally. But for the most part, that is not the objective in treatment.

A (Slaby): One thing that wasn't employed were trials of antidepressants, particularly of monoamine oxidase inhibitors, which sometimes modify or alleviate sustained, long-term depressions. Before a therapist begins to see a patient as hopeless as the patient does, a trial of MAO inhibitors should be provided.

A (Smith): I am not at all clear about what it is that Dr. Hertzman thinks we disagree on. Of course, there are certain ego functions that need to be supported in most therapies, maybe in all analytic situations.

I would add to what I said earlier about how I conceptualize this patient's suicidal behavior. You can think of suicidal behavior as you think of other forms of acting out. It is a resistance and a defense. It is not just to be understood at as superficial a level as something people do when they get depressed.

Against what is suicide a resistance? I believe it is usually a resistance to relinquishing unrealistic core conflicts. Because suicide is an instance of acting out, a therapist is wise to address all events of acting out in therapy. I am reminded of R. J. Langs' (1976) work about "the therapeutic frame" and how important it is to keep such a conceptual frame so that you can detect and analyze small areas of acting out. One area of acting out that occurs with such patients that needs to be actively pursued (and maybe was in this case) is when they call you at home to deal with minor crises. I take up home calls very vigorously with my patients. I do not have very many patients who call me at home, and I don't expect them to do so. If the patient is in the midst of a serious suicidal crisis, I make myself available at that time. But apart from the suicidal crisis, I examine most instances of their acting out with me.

A (Slaby): In emergency psychiatry, there are many factors contributing to burnout. The patients under discussion are very interesting to us. They provide us a window into personality that few other individuals do. But they demand that we set boundaries. The first question we have to ask ourselves is how many patients like this can we carry? To carry a significant number would be a big task. Some therapists cannot set boundaries as well as others. To reduce burnout, therapists in certain clinical settings may share "on call." This provides weekends and certain nights as reprieves from the demands of working with this type of patient. Finally, as has been mentioned, consultation, supervision, or transferring a patient are all worthwhile considerations when dealing with difficult patients. Consultation and supervision are not used enough in seasoned clinician's practices. Sometimes therapists get burned out simply because they just get trapped in an awful situation. They too begin to feel hopeless.

Comment (from audience): I don't have a clear, strong definition of a suicide pact, but I have some ideas to share. I think there are two kinds. One we might call a "tight" suicide pact; the other, "loose." The tight suicide pact, I believe, is based on a shared fantasy about what it means to be dead. The shared fantasy may, in one or both of the partners, be delusional or illusional. That is, two people get together and make a crazy consensus that they are going to get together on the other side or that they will punish some common enemy. It is like a subtype of a folie à deaux. We are given no evidence that these women had a "tight" suicide pact; but they did, I think, have a "loose" pact. It may be that the suicide of Patient C was based on some identification with her friend, if we may call her that, who died before and on the idea that she would find her there on the other side.

As to diagnosis, it seems to me that Patient A was ambivalent, highly impulsive, chronically angry, transiently pyschotic (i.e., her reality testing would break down from time to time); she acted out constantly; she was dysphoric; she was preoccupied with suicide. I would have no difficulty saying she had a borderline personality disorder. And I suspect that the second patient (C) did as well, although, considering that injection of phenothiazine, it is quite possible she had a psychosis in the past.

The question is raised about suicide in borderline patients. There are many different theories in the literature suggesting that completed suicide is not common in uncomplicated borderlines, although suicide attempts and self-mutilations are commonplace. The trouble is that, from time to time, a high proportion of people with borderline personality disorders will develop and meet the criteria for major depressive episodes. The problem in treating these patients is to keep a constant vigilance to note shifts in the mental state, to detect when reality testing is failing and when the depression is taking over. It is at those times that borderline patients are likely to complete suicide.

They also are at increased risk when transference psychoses develop and when they are losing a sustaining object. I think the therapist was quite flexible and quite reasonable in agreeing that she could change to another therapist if that is what she said she had to do. I think there is every indication that Therapist B's countertransference was well managed. But Therapist D "couldn't work with [Patient C]...if she used suicide threats to manipulate him. Consequently, he refused to admit her unless she made some very serious attempt and he had no choice." I think a stance like that is a dare that shows to the patient an untherapeutic and unhelpful, controlling attitude.

Comment (from audience): As Dr. Smith said, suicidal behavior is often a resistance and a defense. That is equally true when a patient bothers the therapist at home by constant phone calls. It is a great resistance. It really works. I wonder if this wasn't preceded by the therapy going very well. In my experience this is an example of the well-known "negative therapeutic reaction"; that is, for various reasons, which I believe are based on family dynamics, the patient has to undermine the therapy and does so very skillfully because of years of experience at doing just that.

With regard to the suicide pact, I am reminded of the paper by David Reiss, "The Suicide Six" (1968). He reported on six patients—all suicidal—on an inpatient ward. Two at a time would get together and instigate each other to commit suicide. Then, spontaneously, they organized themselves into a group. While together as a group, they exhibited no suicidal behavior. One of the strong implications was that when two suicidal people get together, the danger of suicide occurring increases. When three or more get together, a positive or therapeutic effect develops, I believe, because helping or rescuing needs are released.

REFERENCES

Eddy, D. M., Wolpert, R. L., & Rosenberg, M. L. (1987). Estimating the effectiveness of interactions to prevent youth suicides. *Medical Care, 25* (Suppl. 912), 557–565.

Eyman, J. R. (1987, May). *Unsuccessful psychotherapy with seriously suicidal borderline patients.* Paper presented at the 20th Annual Meeting of the American Association of Suicidology, San Francisco.

Friedman, R., Aranoff, M., Clarkin, J., Corn, R., & Hurt, S. W. (1983). History of suicidal behavior in depressed, borderline patients. *American Journal of Psychiatry, 140,* 1023–1026.

Furman, E. (1984). Some difficulties in assessing depression and suicide in childhood. In H. S. Sudak, A. B. Ford, & N. B. Rushforth (Eds.), *Suicide in the young* (pp. 245–258). Boston: John Wright.

Gold, M.S., & Slaby, A. E. (in press). *Dual diagnosis patients.* New York: Marcel-Dekker.

Goldstein, L. S., & Buongiorno, P. A. (1984). Psychotherapists as suicide survivors. *American Journal of Psychotherapy, 38,* 392–398.

Gunderson, J. (1984). *Borderline personality disorder.* Washington, DC: American Psychiatric Press.

Kernberg, O. F. (1984). *Severe personality disorders: Psychotherapeutic strategies.* New Haven, CT: Yale University Press.

Kernberg, O. F. (1987). Projective identification, countertransference and hospital treatment. *Psychiatric Clinics of North America, 10,* 257–272.

Kullgren, G. (1988). Factors associated with completed suicide in borderline personality disorder. *Journal of Nervous and Mental Disease, 176,* 40–44.

Langs, R. J. (1976). *The bipersonal field.* New York: Jason Aronson.

Linehan, M. M. (1987). Dialectic behavior therapy for borderline personality disorder: Theory and method. *Bulletin of the Menninger Clinic, 51,* 261–276.

Litman, R. E. (1965). When patients commit suicide. *American Journal of Psychiatry, 19,* 570–576.

Maltsberger, J. (1986). *Suicide risk: The formulation of clinical judgment.* New York: New York University Press.

Maltsberger, J., & Buie D. (1974). Countertransference hate in the treatment of suicidal patients. *Archives of General Psychiatry, 30,* 625–633.

Masterson, J. F. (1976). *Psychotherapy of the borderline adult: A development approach.* New York: Brunner-Mazel.

McGlashan, T. H. (1987). Borderline personality disorder and unipolar affective disorder: Long-term effects of co-morbidity. *Journal of Nervous and Mental Disease, 175,* 467–473.

Reiss, D. (1968). The suicide six: Observations on suicidal behavior and group function. *International Journal of Social Psychiatry, 14,* 201–212.

Shearer, S. L., Peters, C. P., Quaytman, M. S., & Wadman, B. E. (1988). Intent and lethality of suicide attempts among female borderline inpatients. *American Journal of Psychiatry, 145,* 1424–1427.

Shneidman, E. S. (1985). *Definition of suicide.* New York: John Wiley & Sons.

Silver, D. Cardish, R. J., & Glassman, E. J. (1987). Intensive treatment of characterologically difficult patients. *Psychiatric Clinics of North America, 10,* 219–245.

Slaby, A. E., (1986). Prevention, early identification and management of adolescent suicidal potential. *Rhode Island Medical Journal, 69,* 463–470.

Slaby, A. E. (1989). Emergency psychiatry. In H. I. Kaplan & B. J. Sadock (Eds.),

The comprehensive textbook of psychiatry (5th ed.). Baltimore: Williams and Wilkins.

Stone, M. H. (1980). The suicidal patient: Points concerning diagnosis and intensive treatment. *Psychiatric Quarterly, 52,* 52–70.

Stone, M. H. (1982, April). *Risk factors in suicidal borderlines.* Paper presented at the meeting of the American Association of Suicidology, New York.

Stone, M. H., Stone, D. K., & Hurt, S. W. (1987). Natural history of borderline patients treated by intensive hospitalization. *Psychiatric Clinics of North America, 10,* 185–206.

5

Issues in Therapy and Clinical Management: II

CASE STUDY: THE MAN WITH THE GUN

John, age 32, entered outpatient therapy when his fiancée abruptly terminated their engagement. This 2-year relationship had a decidedly sadomasochistic character, marked by mutual and frequent use of cocaine. In response to the loss of this relationship, John was seriously depressed, enormously ashamed, and preoccupied with thoughts of suicide. His suicide ideation was reminiscent of a time 10 years previously when, in response to the last of a series of rejections from medical schools, he turned on the engine in the family car in a closed garage, only to be interrupted by his parents' unexpected return home. That incident was never discussed in or out of the family.

John lives alone in a home he owns. He is employed as a highly successful salesman whose work requires frequent time "on the road." It is a life-style that suits his desire to live and be alone, although he claims a number of "good friends," none of whom really know him.

John is the second oldest of four children in a professional family. His role in his family of origin (as a child and now) is that of a super-responsible, independent, dependable, and effective adult. It was neither characterologic nor comfortable for him to admit to need or vulnerability. As an example of the pressure to fulfill this expectation, John developed a bleeding ulcer at age 8! Coming to therapy and dealing with his current, intense feelings of loss and incompetence definitively was not his style. In spite of this, he was initially cooperative in interview. It was in these early sessions, in an assessment of his suicidality, that he disclosed that he had a gun at his home. With the therapist's encouragement, John agreed to give the gun to his therapist "for safekeeping."

John maintained in treatment via a fragile alliance for 5 weeks. It was excruciatingly difficult for him to self-disclose and admit to otherwise obvious vulnerabilities. Consequently, progress was slow and the individual sessions quite difficult. Little, if any, change in presenting symptoms was noted, and attempts to suggest medication or hospitalization were steadfastly resisted. At the sixth session, John reported to this therapist that he had decided to stop therapy "because [he] wanted [his] gun returned." He stated that he understood the irrationality of this but that the urge to retrieve his gun was "very strong." Attempts to counteract his demand and decision were met with increasing agitation and threat of legal action.

The presenting issue relates to the treatment of the suicidal but nonaligned resistant patient and specifically to the patient's right to his property versus the therapist's responsibility vis-à-vis the patient's safety. What are the therapeutic and legal ramifications of the therapist's returning the gun or refusing John access to his property? Should the gun be returned to John? If so, how should that be effected?

COMMENTARY

John Maltsberger:

Before taking up questions of how this case might best be managed, I want to mention several points from the case material we have at hand.

I think we have no choice, on the basis of the information given, but to assume that this patient is seriously at risk to kill himself. My inference arises from the following considerations: First, the patient is a 32-year-old single, presumably white, male, which puts him straightaway into a group statistically at risk for suicide. More particularly, because the patient, at age 22, suffered from a serious depression complicated with a significantly dangerous suicide attempt and because he is now depressed again, I would assume that he suffers from a major depressive disorder or what used to be called manic-depressive illness. We know that from 50 to 70% of people who commit suicide bear this diagnosis. Another ominous sign is his history of drug abuse. Furthermore, he is an isolated person. He has no sustaining relationships, no close friendships, except possibly the one he has just lost, which seems to have triggered the present crisis. He has no alliance with his therapist. Not only is there no alliance, but he appears to be treatment-resistant. It has been shown in the literature (Farberow, Shneidman, & Neuringer, 1970; Virkkunen, 1976) that patients who are treatment-resistant are much more likely to die of suicide at some future time. Also of concern is the fact that his family had a disturbing response to his suicide attempt 10 years ago. As Joseph Richman (1971) has shown us, suicide very often is a cooperative effort between the patient who does it and the people in the social network around him. That the family paid no attention before is chilling.

Although the case material is sketchy, I infer that this suicide-vulnerable man has managed to keep himself in some kind of equilibrium by relying on the exterior support he was able to derive from his finacée, who has now left him, and on the bolstering of self-esteem that his work success has provided. It is important to note that it was a work disappointment—rejection from medical school—that precipitated the first suicide attempt. We know that John is vulnerable to work disappointments and disappointments in love.

The foregoing details, coupled with the information that the patient has been preoccupied with suicide, possesses a gun that is now a point of contention, has been unable to form a therapeutic alliance, and is now leaving treatment are quite enough to satisfy me that this patient is a serious danger to himself and that the unenviable therapist must deal with a dangerous suicidal crisis.

The situation may be even more grave, as the possibility exists of a developing paranoid breakdown. We must bear in mind that John is not capable of forming a relationship of trust and that he may be preoccupied with much that is hidden from view. At first, the patient seemed hopeful and cooperative, but he grew angry and difficult. Now he threatens legal action. The slightest sign of a formal thought disorder, a clang or loose association, blocking, ideas of reference, some minute autistic or bizarre detail in the patient's speech or manner would suggest to me that the patient is suffering from a paranoid psychosis. We know that seriously depressed patients, when delusional, are five times more likely to commit suicide than those who are not. Furthermore, if the patient is paranoid, he is much more likely to be influenced by his own unrealistic preoccupations and beliefs than he is by any well-meant verbal interventions by his therapist. He may be dominated by secret beliefs concerning the afterlife that we know nothing about and that make suicide extraordinarily attractive to him.

Finally, we must bear in mind the possibility that the patient may not only be a danger to himself but a danger to others as well. Is he, for instance, planning to shoot the woman who has thrown him over before he shoots himself? Has he developed a psychotic conviction that the therapist is out to get him, so that he intends to shoot the therapist before shooting himself?

Even though it may be difficult to tell whether the patient is harboring a hidden psychosis, I would conclude that in the absence of a therapeutic alliance, with the announced intention of leaving treatment, and with the demand for the return of the gun, the patient intended to kill at least himself, and I would arrange for an involuntary hospitalization.

Not that involuntary hospitalization might not, for the moment at least, make matters worse. Forced hospitalization might well interfere with the patient's work, and we know that work disappointment dashed his self-esteem so severely 10 years ago that he tried to asphyxiate himself. Furthermore, a forced hospitalization would likely make any further work with the present therapist quite impossible. But the alternative, the patient's suicide, is much worse. There might be another job, another therapist, even another woman somewhere in the future, but not if there is no future.

I view John's demand that the gun be returned in the context of leaving treatment as an unconscious plea for the therapist to take the responsibility for getting him into the hospital even though consciously the patient might be very afraid of it. Maneuvering of this sort is commonplace in paranoid cases. For the therapist to hand the gun over to John would be tantamount to saying, "Go ahead, then, and shoot yourself."

What if, on the other hand, the therapist were to refuse to return the gun and insist on hospital admission? John almost certainly would protest, but the therapist would then have placed himself unambiguously on the side of the patient's not committing suicide.

Certainly, the patient's behavior suggests that although suicide is a dangerous possibility, he has not yet finally decided to put an end to his life. Presumably, John must have had a firearms permit in the first place in order to obtain the gun. He could get another and kill himself with it forthwith, or commit suicide by jumping or poisoning. Instead, he chooses to pick a fight with his therapist, ostensibly over the question of who should have the gun. In fact, I think the patient is setting up a struggle about who is going to take responsibility for his living or dying. I believe this patient is asking his therapist the question: "Will you stop me?"

May I add that I am not comfortable with the fact that the therapist had taken custody of the gun in the first place? I do not have a firearms permit, and in Massachusetts at least, to have a gun in one's possession without a permit is a felony that carries with it a mandatory sentence of a year in prison. So I would not have taken custody of the gun, or at least not for very long. Had the patient refused to get rid of his gun—either by giving it to the police, selling it, or handing it over to some other responsible person in the first place, I might have accepted it but only long

enough to go to the nearest police station and hand it in. In my own practice I have persuaded a patient to sell all of his firearms, to bring me the
receipt from the gun store to show me he had done so, and then to give
me his gun permit to keep for him, making it difficult to replace the
original weapons.

This is what I would do in John's case. I would once again urge John
to accept hospitalization on a voluntary basis, which I presume he would
refuse. I would then tell him that I could not return his gun because I
feared he would try to kill himself with it but that if he wanted to take
the matter to a lawyer, I would be glad to talk with the lawyer about it.
If John had seemed sufficiently excitable, angry, and paranoid to me in
the past, I would be at some pains to tell him this in a secure setting where
I would feel safe in case of an attempted assault. I would then tell the patient I would see him again in the very near future—I would hope the next
day—to talk the matter over further.

I would then arrange to have an ambulance wait near my office at the
time of the next appointment, without telling John about it. I would also
arrange with the ambulance company to have four strong attendants
waiting out of sight on the premises, on the presumption that John might
require forcible restraint to get to the hospital. When the patient returned for his appointment, I would urge him to accept voluntary hospitalization; and if he refused to go voluntarily, I would say, "Well, I am going
to send you to the hospital." I would then sign a certificate testifying that
I thought he was a serious danger to himself and possibly to others and
have him restrained and carried out to the waiting ambulance.

At that time I would inform the family of waht I had done, and then
I would deliver the gun personally to the nearest police station.

Although these maneuvers seem extreme, I think the circumstances
justify them. To threaten the patient with involuntary hospitalization
would be a mistake, in my view, because that would invite him to take
flight. Saying to the patient, "I'll commit you to the hospital if you won't
go voluntarily," conveys the message "Run now if you will, or kill yourself
now, because you are going to be overpowered and carried away." Threats
to force hospitalization really are like blackmail. They invite patients to
get into a power struggle with the therapist.

One might argue that forcing this man into the hospital will ruin the
therapy. I would answer that there isn't any therapy going on now. There
is no alliance here, no engagement between the therapist and the patient.
So I can imagine two possible scenarios. First, once in the hospital, the
patient might say that the therapist was a monster. He then might find
someone else in the hospital who would be the good guy, so to speak.
He might be driven into an alliance in this way. The other possiblity is
that the patient might cool off after being furious and decide that perhaps
the therapist had really saved his life, and he might then form a

therapeutic alliance. I once had a university professor dragged, scream-ing, out of my consulting room under just these circumstances. He was hospitalized, involuntarily and treated. That was 10 years ago. I still get a Christmas card from him each and every year in which he says, "Thank you."

Sam Heilig:

This is a very complex issue. A high-risk suicidal patient comes to therapy and then wants to leave before treatment has had any effect. The therapist is in a difficult dilemma; the patient can't be forced to come to treatment, and the therapist can't simply let the case go. Does the therapist have an obligation to hospitalize this man, against his will, because he is a danger to himself? If the patient simply stops coming and then commits suicide, is the therapist exposed to a suit for not having taken action to prevent the suicide? How do we break through the resistance and defensive posture of a high-risk suicidal man, threatening to withdraw from therapy? What do we do about the gun? We can't give it back and still have a good night's sleep.

First, as his therapist I would explicitly give him my evaluation. This is a serious, life-or-death matter. His life is at stake. His response to the loss of his fiancée has caused a strong reaction, and he is not himself. I might say something like "You are in the midst of a nervous breakdown, and it is necessary that you have treatment."

Second, his therapist should outline his or her responsibility to in-tervene. In a case where there is a "danger to self" the doctor has both a professional, ethical imperative and a possible legal obligation to in-tervene once the case is brought to professional care. The point here is to accent the therapist's concern about the seriousness of the case and the intention to actively intervene to help. The patient might be told that he is not functioning at his usual level and needs to rely on the judgment of people who want to help him. If he wants to consult with another therapist, I would assist him in that. This gives him an opportunity to take some action and a bit of control. Consulting another professional also has the likelihood of confirming his need for treatment.

During this crisis phase of the therapy, I would insist to John that I must involve his family. There are several reasons for this. This man may leave treatment and then will need as much support as he can muster. He would be unlikely to seek it out himself, but families can impose themselves to help.

The family can also provide information about the patient that may not be available directly or possibly about other episodes of disturbances and how they were resolved. The therapist would have an opportunity to observe the family's interaction style. Sometimes, in an acute crisis, old defensive patterns break down and communication is more direct, revealing, and helpful.

The therapist also shares the burden of responsibility with the family; I usually have found that this provides some relief to my own anxiety in such cases. Appraising the family of the patient's role and involving them in the process of helping diminishes the possibility of being sued by the family should this patient kill himself.

John's family may have additional ideas as to planning a course of treatment or care that might be more acceptable to him. For example, if the gun is to be returned, it might be much easier to give it to John's parents than to give it to John. If John did stop treatment, I would keep the door open by continuing my involvement with the family, who still have the problem of how to help John. This may allow John some time to reconsider and return to treatment.

Most important, in a case such as this, it is reassuring to feel you are not on your own. This family would probably want to do what appears to be the correct thing and would in all likelihood cooperate with the therapist.

Also, John should be told that there are two phases of his problem and the need for therapy. First there is the immediate crisis of his imminent suicide danger that must be dealt with as an emergency to protect his life. Second, there is the question of what got him into this predicament. There was a similar serious suicidal episode 10 years earlier when he was rejected from medical school. I would point up his particular vulnerability to feelings of inadequacy or incompetence, which brings him to suicide. I would remind him of the fact that he got himself through it. He probably is reacting to similar dynamics now and should have long-term therapy to understand what it is in him that brings him to such a desperate state when he feels a sense of failure. I would give him the hope that therapy can teach him how to understand himself and have better control of his feelings and his life. The main point to this is to look beyond the immediate crisis and realistically offer hope to resolve his underlying problem with therapy.

I would enumerate his strengths. He is very strong in work, is independent, owns his own home, can have relationships that mean a lot to him. What went wrong? Why does he have this terrible reaction to a loss? He needs to understand these dynamics. At age 32, there will be other relationships, and he should learn how to make his life work in a more gratifying way.

Who is to possess the gun poses a legal issue that is rather intriguing and deceptive. The easy argument is to assume simply that John has a right to his personal property. This is highly questionable in this circumstance. As mentioned earlier, if the gun is returned and John commits suicide with it, the therapist might be sued for malpractice. John is in a disturbed state and a danger to himself and clearly should not have the gun.

One possible approach would be to encourage John to test his legal rights to demand the gun and to sue the therapist for the return of his personal property. This has many interesting and helpful ramifications. It involves John in a contest to demand his rights and may divert him from his suicidal thoughts and depression. It extends the time of action indefinitely if John can involve himself in a legal process. It also emphasizes the therapist's judgment about the seriousness of John's situation and his willingness to actively intervene.

If John does sue for his gun, the therapist cannot incur any damages that I can foresee, beyond the cost or inconvenience of responding to the legal process, that is, attorney's fees and court costs. Even if the court decided the gun must be returned to John (which would be an interesting question to test), he did not suffer any material damages.

In a case as unusual as this, in which the therapist's anxiety would be high, it is advisable for the therapist to seek consultation. Any high-risk suicide case makes everyone anxious—family, friends, co-workers, doctors, neighbors, and certainly therapists, who find themselves with a responsibility involving life or death. It is reassuring, clarifying, and ultimately beneficial to the patient as well if the therapist consults with colleagues.

Robert Yufit:

Entangled in this case vignette are a number of ethical, moral, therapeutic, and legal issues. Many of the answers we may arrive at are not going to be clear-cut.

First and most important, the gun should not be returned to John even though it is his property. The gun cannot be returned to John because, in my assessment, it is very likely to be used in another suicide attempt. John clearly is a high suicide risk.

I base my assessment of his suicide risk on a number of factors: his personality structure, which I consider to be vulnerable to suicidal behavior; his abuse of drugs, especially cocaine; and his history of a prior, highly lethal suicide attempt, which was unexpectedly interrupted by his parents' return. He has neither an adequate external social network nor usable internal resources at this time. Consistent with this, he also has never talked to anyone about his prior suicide attempt, and the lack of trust implied in being unable to share is considered to be an ominous sign.

Coupled with his strong desire to have a lethal weapon returned to his possession, there is the current stress of an apparent perceived failure in therapy. At this point, John is viewing therapy as yet another failure to which he is expressing a desire to respond with a behavior that parallels that of 10 years ago, that is, his first suicide attempt when he failed to gain entrance to medical school. These are powerful historical and therapeutic reasons for deciding not to return his gun to him.

I believe the therapist made a mistake in the first place in deciding to take the gun for so-called safekeeping. That decision established the power struggle that is now being played out. Having taken the gun, however, it is imperative that the therapist now not return the gun to John. Not returning the gun protects both the individual (John) from himself and society from the individual. It also reflects an attitude of caring on the part of the therapist. There may be some legal issues involved regarding John's rights to property (I talked with an attorney friend about this case, and he was unsure what legal rights this patient would have in such a situation), but the ethical, moral, and therapeutic issues clearly supersede the possible legal rights of property of the patient. I feel strongly that the preservation of life clearly is a higher-order concern than are rights of ownership and believe that the court would rule in favor of the therapist should John initiate a suit. In fact, initiating a suit might be a good opportunity for John to develop an ongoing, future-oriented activity and diffuse somewhat the more active suicide possibilities.

The therapist is clearly protected by the existing codes of ethics of the major mental health disciplines in not returning a lethal weapon to a suicidal person. This is particularly the case regarding issues of confidentiality under conditions of threat to life. John's risk for acting on his suicide ideation is sufficiently high that the therapist could, for example and as one alternative, return the gun to a family member with a full explanation of the situation.

What are the ramifications of such an action? Such an act could destroy the therapeutic relationship. But since not much of a relationship has developed thus far anyway, this may not be of great concern. On the other hand, giving the gun to a family member, in order to both keep the gun safe and to ensure John's safety by keeping the gun from him, might create further opportunity to discuss issues of control, issues that certainly need further therapeutic attention.

It is, of course, highly desirable to try to preserve what remains of the therapeutic relationship. Discussing the challenge that John has posed to this therapist, as well as the underlying elements of John's control and feelings of worthlessness, may provide further basis for interaction between John and his therapist. One would hope that as a consequence more constructive involvement would follow. Engaging John in any kind of ongoing activity will help develop a much needed future time perspective, which is so necessary to gain the time to establish and develop a critically needed and workable therapeutic alliance.

Even before a decision about the gun is made, it would be useful therapeutically to discuss fully with John what his current status really is. Rather than make any assumptions, I would want to ask why he wants to stop therapy now. Is this another attempt to perpetuate failure? Why does he want the gun back? Even though the answer to this last question seems rather obvious, I wonder whether he has other intentions. What is his plan? Is he playing a power game with the therapist? We really do not know the answers to these questions. Although not returning the gun to John seems so obviously the right decision to make, discussing his intentions with him would give us a further chance to discern what John really wants and would give us, I think, a basis for dealing with any legal complications that might arise in deciding not to return the gun to him at this time.

Because John is described as having been "initially cooperative" in therapy, the therapist needs to determine what has caused the rapid decline of the potential therapeutic alliance. Especially important, what were the factors contributing to the establishment of the initially good rapport. Is this a fear of commitment to therapy? Is this illustrative of his sado-masochistic character structure and/or is the therapeutic relationship one more sado-masochistic relationship, similar to those John has fostered in the past? My point is that John's needs for control are paramount issues for exploration in his psychotherpy, and if these can be resolved now, the decision about returning the gun becomes moot.

If John is incapable of addressing these issues, or should he become more adamant or agitated, I would propose that commitment as a psychiatric inpatient would be warranted as a necessary safeguard for all concerned: John, his former fiance, the therapist, and family members. State statutes regarding commitment may differ, but the therapist's responsibility is to John's safety and the protection of society. Again, the possibility of harm to others, should the gun be returned to John, cannot be ruled out. Thus, if John appears unlikely to be maintained in psychotherapy, which, as currently described, does not seem to be a favorable prospect, notification of his parents may well be indicated. The hospital milieu will help prevent easy accessibility to lethal weapons and should minimize acting out of self-destructive behaviors. Possibly, in the greater safety of this therapeutic milieu, these issues can be explored and insightfully worked through; and the consequent threat of self-harm or destructive behavior, to himself and others, will be considerably lessened.

Most important, the inpatient milieu should provide needed time and more external control to facilitate getting to "know" John, by the therapist and hospital staff, something even his "good friends have been unable to do." A missing link in the entire picture is that of trust. A lack of trust is present in all directions, especially between John and his therapist. Establishing such trust is a key psychodynamic in understanding and controlling this dilemma and ultimately in preventing a suicide or a homicide from taking place.

Questions and Responses

Commentary (Yufit): Dr. Maltsberger has remarked that, in his view, this patient is not currently in psychotherapy. I disagree. In a strictly formal sense he is correct. There is no evidence of a trusting therapeutic alliance. But I believe there definitely is a therapeutic struggle going on, a struggle for control. I think that John is really challenging the therapist to do something. He's asking, "Who is most powerful?", "How much do you care?" or "What do you want to do?" I think this is an aspect of therapy that we should not overlook as important. As has been pointed out, John could at any time have chosen to leave therapy and complete his suicide. So far he has not made that choice.

A (Maltsberger): That is fair enough. The patient certainly is trying to undertake some negotiation with the therapist. I think he is saying, "Save my life if you can." I would not be slow to respond.

Q: Would any of you have sought consultation about this case? If so, with whom and at what point?

A (Yufit): I would have. I would consult with a trusted, well-informed colleague who was available. I would advise anybody to consult a colleague regarding any difficult and anxiety-laden, legally complicated case.

A (Heilig): I always do, partly because I am not always sure I can think rationally in a situation as heated as this. There are other good reasons for seeking consultation. More important, I want to minimize the likelihood that I would have to face a jury in a courtroom on charges of negligence. I consult, and I put the gist of that consultation in my notes. That documented consultation is evidence of my intent to provide the best possible treatment.

A (Maltsberger): I would consult as much to avoid possible charges of negligence as to deal with my own anxiety. I think that any time I get into a difficult case, where I am concerned that somebody is imminently suicidal, as I think this man is, I would want to be careful. It is enormously helpful to ask a colleague to help to monitor one's own judgment when in a tense, anxiety-provoking situation.

Audience comment: I want to make two points. First, that not giving back the gun in some sense might start therapy. As has been pointed out, this patient might appropriately interpret this as a caring behavior. It would convey to the patient that you give a damn. Second, I would urge us to look at the antecedents. What kind of transference was involved before this patient regressed? Did the therapist, perhaps just like the patient's family, convey a message of hopelessness to this patient, giving, or at least accentuating, permission to die or to kill himself?

I think one of the factors that makes it impossible to give back the gun is that the gun has now become the therapist's gun. As Dr. Maltsberger has pointed out in much of his writings, patients often have other scenarios worked out. One of those scenarios is "You haven't save me; you've killed me." Right now that gun is a loaded gun. It no longer is just a gun that might be returned. It is a gun that has been in the hands of the therapist and about which there have been discussions. I think that more focus has to be put upon the fact that this case was mishandled from the beginning. It is now being presented as though this patient requires hospitalization, as he well may at this particular point. Maybe he would in any case; nobody can say that for sure. But my experience is that the most serious suicidal patients will link to you by trying to frighten you with the idea of their death. That is the way they use a suicide image in their therapy. They are going to scare the life out of you; if they can, they will control the therapy. This therapist clearly was scared from the beginning. Everything the therapist is now asking (should he be hospitalized? can I get him medication? can I get his gun away?) demonstrates the therapist's anxiety. I think that when suicidal patients get therapists into a position where the therapist is more responsible for the patient's life than the patient is, therapy is out of control. So at the point at which we are presented with this dilemma, there is no good solution. Therapy cannot be preserved anymore. The only solution about which you are all speaking is in terms of preserving life, not therapy.

I worked for about 5 years with Vietnam veterans. A large number of them were suicidal; all of them had guns. You could not begin to involve them in therapy if you made it a condition of therapy that they would have to give up their gun. Also, most of them were either suicidal or potentially homicidal, and they talked about it. I agree with you that progress in therapy is measured by when they give up the gun. I agree that voluntary surrender of the gun is the ideal solution. But for the patient, that is a form of surrender. I would not make it a condition of therapy that I would not treat somebody unless that person surrendered a weapon. I would be discussing the gun and the need to relate to me in that way, the need to try to transfer anxiety to me.

Would it not be appropriate and better for the therapeutic relationship to have the patient surrender the gun to the police rather than to the therapist?

A (Heilig): Two issues are immediately posed by this patient's possession of a gun. The primary issue is to get the gun away from a highly suicidal patient. I wouldn't care much who took it—a friend, a family member, the police, or a hock shop—just that he got rid of it. The second issue is the meaning of the gun within the patient's therapy. It has all kinds of symbolic meaning, and it has to be assessed in terms of the quality of the therapeutic alliance. I believe that to deprive a suicidal patient who volunteers to give you his proposed and available suicide method, his pills, gun, or other means, has a lot of positive therapeutic promise.

Q: But he can always find something else. We see that he tried to commit suicide by carbon monoxide 10 years ago. He could go home and overdose.

A (Heilig): That is, of course, true. But I don't think it works that way. This man may certainly have access to pills. If he lives in a large city, he can certainly jump off the roof of a building. There are many things he can do; but he has not chosen to use these methods. Instead, he is asking for his gun back.

A (Yufit): The point is that he is asking for his gun back, rather than using another method. I think this very much implies the importance of the ongoing and potential therapeutic struggle—engaging with the therapist.

I am concerned about the use of the gun as a means of communication. If you look at the brief history we have on this gentleman, it seems that he used cocaine to communicate in his relationship with his girl friend, and he attempted to use carbon monoxide to communicate with his parents. I am wondering if we could view this, his gun, as his attempt at getting some kind of therapeutic alliance between himself and his therapist. Perhaps his talking about the gun is his way of trying to open up some communication. I am concerned that we may overattend to the gun as a lethal weapon rather than as a very important symbolic communication, which, if attended to as such, could open up something very valuable for this patient.

A (Heilig): I was thinking in similar terms when I spoke of encouraging John to get into a legal action—to sue me to get his gun back. That forces him to talk with his therapist, and it might focus his therapy.

A (Maltsberger): Certainly, to return the gun would be contraindicated. Clinically, it would also increase your liability. I spoke to a lawyer about this case before the conference. He agreed that one would be liable for gross negligence in a malpractice action if one gave the gun back. Relying merely on the information that we have, this patient seems so dangerous to me that I would prefer all of these discussions to take place in a protected setting. Certainly, if the patient were to sue me to force the return of the gun, for false arrest, for mayhem because I caused my agents to lay hold of him—any or all of those legal actions would be fine. But I have some concern about the family. It is too bad we do not have more information about the family. The information provided suggests that they absolutely ignored a very dangerous episode. If one tried to deal with this man and his family in an outpatient setting, the family might join forces with him and resist a necessary hospitalization.

Q: I recognize this is frequently a problem when you deal with a fictionalized case, but one of the concerns I have about the discussion thus far is that we are losing sight of the person—the patient. I myself have not been involved in accepting a gun from a patient, but I have accepted razor blades, well recognizing that they can be purchased again; aspirin, well recognizing it can be purchased again; and assorted pills, well recognizing that the prescriptions were still outstanding and that there was no way I could further protect the person.

I have been involved as well in a situation in which a woman wound up ultimately making three fairly dangerous suicide attempts in spite of the fact that hospitalizations and medication and psychiatric and psychological consultations were involved. All of them were essentially made, in one way or another, at my doorstep. Many of my colleagues were concerned about why I wasn't very upset at what was happening. What I was mostly concerned about, and was trying to ascertain, was what she was trying to communicate to me. Finally, through some dreams that she was able to recount, she started to be able to tap into some early childhood sexual activity. I am still unsure whether we were talking about actual incest or molestation or "merely" some type of emotional overstimulation with which she was unable to deal at the ages of 4, 5, and 6. Given the trauma that resulted, she had to seal this off. It was buried inside and became the basis for some characterological difficulties that she continues to struggle with even now, well into her mid-40s. Once that festering boil was opened up, metaphorically, the suicidal ideation continued for a little while and then completely disappeared. Currently, she is at a point where she no longer has thoughts of suicide. It has been 5 months. I am aware of the time because the patient is aware of it; she keeps marking her progress: "I am not worrying about that anymore"; and by the way she talks about it, she is really thinking of things in a different way.

I want also to add a true story and to ask a question. In regard to giving the gun back, there is no need to ask a lawyer. I will cite the case of

Freddie Prinze, who had been in therapy for a long time with a psychiatrist in Los Angeles, who had taken Prinze's gun at Prinze's request. On a given day, when Freddie asked for it back, the doctor gave it back. Prinze shot himself with that gun. The out-of-court settlement in that case was for a half million dollars. Now the question is; would your reactions be the same if this was a chronically suicidal person? The case begins with the word "abruptly." It is a crisis case, and we are immediately put in a rescuing mode. Suppose this man had been depressed recurrently, had been in the hospital several times, and had been in therapy for quite a long time, would that in any way change your attitude about its management.

A (Maltsberger): It very well might. I still would not give the gun back. But there are cases in which there is some therapeutic alliance that is holding the patient back from suicide, and forcing hospitalization would destroy it. Some clever patients can go into a hospital and in a few days convince the staff that there is no longer a danger of suicide. I would not force hospitalization in circumstances where what alliance there was would be destroyed and where the therapeutic relationship was essential for keeping the patient alive.

I had a case of an aging professional man who was extremely socially isolated. He had guns, and he would go out into the woods with a pistol, put it in his mouth, and click the trigger, knowing the chamber was empty, as a rehearsal of his suicide. I did succeed in having him get rid of his gun; he was the person whose gun permit I had. But in some way or another, the patient got another one. It was perfectly plain to me that if I had put him in the hospital, that would have been it. He said, "You can put me in the hospital. But I will be out in three days, and you will never see me again." There are circumstances where a forced hospitalization, particularly of a chronic, long-standing suicidal patient, can actually precipitate what you want to avoid. So what I did in that case was to have extensive consultation. The patient was in the middle of a divorce. He gave me permission to speak to his lawyer about the circumstances of his divorce. I was able to talk to the lawyer and to give a warning to the wife through both his lawyer and the judge. The patient was thinking of shooting his wife before he shot himself. Sometimes you have to manage without the hospital.

A (Heilig): You present a case different from the one we are dealing with, that is, a man who is withdrawing from treatment. As I understand your case, you have a man coming to treatment with a long history of this kind of problem. What I would do with such a case is take advantage of the obvious feature of his coming for help. My approach is different when a patient comes asking for help. I would extensively review his history in terms of what helped him in the past. He has been through episodes like this before, and, based on his history, I would want to find a method that would be acceptable to him. That is the kind of help I would want to extend, whether it is hospitalization, drug therapy, psychotherapy, or simply a change of scene. Whatever has worked in the past is what I would look for. It is a quite different kind of attitude. I would slow everything down. It is no longer an urgent situation. If it is a long-term, repeated problem, the urgencies are quite different.

Q: This patient has engaged in the mutual and frequent use of cocaine. As we all know, the withdrawal and the depression that occurs from cocaine can be extremely devastating to an individual, causing suicidal feelings as well as financial pressures, which in time may lead to more suicidal tendencies. Could you address the issues posed by his use of and withdrawal from cocaine? Would you address that at all in your therapy with this patient?

A (Yufit): This is a very interesting and important issue. We are not told whether John is currently on cocaine. If he is on cocaine, I am reminded of the whole issue of developing some form of deferring action. I am particularly intrigued by the notion of getting this person involved in some kind of activity, a lawsuit, or anything at all to promote some level of continuing therapeutic engagement. If we knew whether the person is currently involved in the use of cocaine, I think it would make a big difference in terms of possibly determining if there is an underlying, drug-induced latent psychosis as well.

A (Maltsberger): If this patient has chronic cocaine intoxication, it makes the situation even more dangerous.

Q: I work as a social worker in a high school. There are situations at the high school for which we have to make immediate decisions to attempt to prevent a student from taking his or her life. The situations posed by this case are not always going to occur just in clinical settings. I had one case in which a young woman with whom I was working came into my office while under the influence of alcohol. The potential weapon in her case was her car, which she was going to use to take her life along with that of another person with whom she was very angry. We ended up taking her to the hospital. As the emergency personnel took her away, she cussed and cursed me with every imaginable expletive. Within an hour at the hospital the bond that had been forged was beginning to emerge again. So in the longer run, both her life and her therapy were preserved.

A (Yufit): I understand. I certainly think that not returning the gun clearly conveys the therapist's attitude—the attitude that "Yes, I do care and I do not want you to do anything to yourself."

A (Maltsberger and Heilig): I agree.

Q: If it turns out to be the case, as Dr. Maltsberger has suggested, that this person is psychotic and maybe even delusional, what would be the consequences of suggesting that this man regain power by pursuing a legal action to get the gun back? Therapeutically, is it a good idea to foster the seeds of a delusion that he might regain power, only later to have to deal with the reality that this is a way that will not return power to him?

A (Heilig): If psychotic symptoms were present and emerged during the course of my discussions with John, I think they would have to be dealt with, preferably with medication. I tend not to see evidence for psychosis in this case; but I would certainly want to keep an eye out for it. I think you have a rather obsessive-compulsive, organized man who is trying to maintain control of something. If that began to fragment and psychosis appeared, I would think about other things to do. I would be very careful about having him pursue legal actions under those circumstances.

A (Maltsberger): Given the protocol here, I see no reason to infer that the patient is psychotic. There is enough material to alert me to the possibility of psychosis, however.

A (Yufit): I think that getting the patient involved in some kind of legal activity provides much needed deferring action. I want to buy some time here, to try to reestablish, if at all possible, some kind of working therapeutic alliance. It may not be possible, but I think that the more time I have the better chance I have to work through some of these issues with John.

Q: I have been thinking about an issue that was covered earlier and that seems to me to be the central question. We have here a therapist encouraging a cocaine-abusing and—I think we are in agreement—quite dangerous fellow to bring a gun into the treatment room. Surely, that provides the therapist with a very piquant moment. What might that situation be about? Why would a therapist expose himself to such a situation? Who is the suicidal one here?

A (Heilig): In Los Angeles a fairly large percentage of the population uses cocaine. I think that goes on all over the country. Some cocaine users are suicidal. I don't know that they are dangerous, if that is the implication of your comment.

A (Maltsberger): We don't really have enough data to answer your question. If it were plain that this man was a serious cocaine abuser, that he was in a chronic state of intoxication and had been behaving in a way that is more obviously menacing than we are told, I'd be very scared. But we do not have that data and must read something into the case to infer that.

A (Heilig): The kind of case I would be worried about would not be the cocaine abuser but rather one that we see more frequently, that is an alcohol abuser who is impulse-ridden and unpredictable. Getting involved in therapy with such a person who is suicidal and has a gun would worry me a great deal.

Q: The tension in the relationship between the therapist and the patient, as it is presented, is posed by the patient's demand, "Give me back my gun." Would any of you consider tossing the gun, that is, going down to a river and throwing it away? Then, it is no longer an object of power or control. And if you did, hypothetically, what do you think would happen in the relationship between you and the patient? The gun is no longer available as a source of conflict. The therapist would simply respond, "It's gone. I don't know where it is."

A (Heilig): I like the idea. The only thing he could sue me for was the cost of the gun.

A (Yufit): I don't like the idea. For me, the gun still serves as a focus to promote the power struggle. I want to keep the patient involved, and I would be worried that in a situation like this, because of his previous history, the patient really would leave the therapy. I am trying to promote the therapeutic relationship or whatever is left of it.

A (Maltsberger): To be repetitive, I would use what powers of persuasion and interpretation I have to persuade the patient to return the gun to a gun shop and to give me his gun permit. I think this has the same effect, yet it makes it harder for him to get any other gun.

Q: I have done about 100 intakes involving cocaine using/abusing patients in the past 6 months. We don't have the information in the case write-up on how much cocaine John was using. In my experience, John fits the typical description of a cocaine abuser: he's a salesman, he's young, he's aggressive in a field where there are high expectations, and he has to perform. Cocaine abusers who come in with suicidal ideations do so because they have hit rock bottom. They want to give up cocaine, but they can't seem to make it. For 2 weeks or so they are fine. Then they are back on cocaine, and the suicidal thoughts are running rampant again. What concerns me about this case is, was there an evaluation done at the time? Sometimes you have to deal with the habit before you can deal with the issues involved. Finally, I agree that you have to have family intervention as well. Sometimes there is another family member abusing drugs, and in order to have a plan and treat your patient, acquiring that information is essential.

A (Heilig): One of the things I would have been interested in (and it is not available here) is more information regarding the breakup of the relationship with the girl friend. Is it final, or do they still each feel a great deal of ambivalence? Very often people become suicidal in the ambivalent phase of a breakup. If the woman was still involved in some way, sort of in and out of the relationship with John, I would want to get her involved and evaluate if there was any possibility of reconstructing the relationship.

A (Yufit): We can't underestimate this man. He may want the gun back to use on her.

Q: I am the assistant director of a psychiatric liaison service, and I see a lot of children under a lot of stress. One point that has not been addressed yet is the fact that this young man had a bleeding ulcer at the age of 8. We don't know whether it was treated or not. The case write-up also mentioned that this child was never allowed to be vulnerable. My point is that you cannot get anywhere until you get to that family and get that family involved—to assess that family, to see if they want to be involved, or whether John is/was an expendable child (Sabbath, 1969). If that were so, then maybe the approach would be a little bit different.

A (Maltsberger): I would infer that we enter this case sort of in midstream. A crisis has developed over a period of some weeks. But certainly, when patients are this disturbed, when there is such serious suicide potential, the family should be interviewed. I would take a history from the family as well as from the patient. It is a good idea to do so when there has already been a significant suicide attempt. You need to know where you stand with the family and what kind of people they are. It is possible that if John's family were emotionally more available than I fear, this crisis might have been averted by effective and early family intervention. I make it a fairly regular practice, when I am treating suicidal people, to get the family into old-fashioned case work, which these days is sometimes called family therapy. Sometimes more than one person in the family has to be treated.

Q: I am a consultant at a rehabilitation center. Admitted to our facility was a young, very antisocial person with a long history of alcohol and polydrug abuse, who became paraplegic from a fall. After he was there for a few weeks, he told his nurse that because his sexual functioning was no longer going to be what it was, there was no sense in living and that there was a bullet in his room with his name on it. His nurse reported that to me, and I said we would go check. We did and, lo and behold, there was a .38 caliber bullet in his nightstand. We didn't find any gun. Of course, we confiscated the bullet and notified hospital authorities. The nurse and I were reprimanded for searching the patient's room without his permission! I wanted to ask your thoughts about that. What should we have done with the bullet and the administrator?

A (Maltsberger): It was perfectly proper to search that patient's room.

A (Heilig): I would agree and suggest that you just have to work things out with your administration, as we all do.

Q: I agree with those who feel that the case was mishandled from the very beginning. I respectfully submit that asking the patient to bring in the weapon or the instrument with which he intends to commit suicide does not form a therapeutic alliance but rather an unhealthy and perhpas antitherapeutic coalition. It gives the control of the therapy entirely to the patient. From the very beginning he is making a statement about how he is going to participate in treatment and how he is going to regulate his suicidal impulses. Also, it creates a distraction in which the therapist is busy keeping track of how many pills or knives the patient has and where they are in his drawers. Real issues of his suicidality may not be addressed properly. I also think it creates a false sense of security. Obviously, the patient could go and find some alternative ways of killing himself. I am sure that if the patient came in and produced the weapon and told any practitioner that, instead of killing himself he actually intended to kill somebody else, we would not be satisfied with keeping the weapon. Under the Tarasoff precedent (*Tarasoff v. Regents of University of California*, 1974) we would have to do something other than just keep the weapon. I would not be surprised if someday it will be ruled in some court that by accepting a patient's suicidal weapon, we are acknowledging that he is extremely suicidal. And at the same time, we are acknowledging that we are not doing anything else to effectively treat that condition.

A (Yufit): Let me pose my response through a question, actually a series of questions. Why isn't John considering, at this point, some other method of suicide? After all we do know that at one time he used a car to attempt poisoning himself by carbon monoxide and that an unexpected rescue by his parents took place. This means that he had a heightened suicide potential at that time. So why isn't John now considering some other method? What really is his intention? I am uncertain whether we will have any chance to explore this with him. As we are questioning the quality of the therapeutic alliance, it is reasonable to wonder whether he is going to come back after this session. There are some very important issues about other obviously available methods that we are also not con- sidering. What really are his intentions and his motivations? Does he really want his gun back in order to kill himself, or is there some other reason? Certainly, this needs exploration.

A (Maltsberger): With respect to the point you made about who is responsible for the patient's living and dying, ultimately, of course, the success of treatment rests with the suicidal patient. The goal of therapy should move to the position in which the patient can fairly well take responsibility for his or her own life. The issue of who is responsible for the patient's body is played out in every psychotherapy of people with borderline personality disorders. These people very often talk suicide for manipulative purposes and are not genuinely suicidal, although they may be inclined to maim and mutilate themselves in one way or another. It is sometimes necessary in the beginning of the treatment to take responsibility insofar as one can to protect the patient from himself. Later on there comes a time in the treatment when the therapist has to face the music and say, "Okay, now you have to take over. I am not going to respond to threats anymore." This one can do when there is a strong therapeutic relationship and an alliance. I had one patient who regularly would cut herself in my washroom and leave blood in the basin to punish me for my refusal to get into a control fandango with her. She wanted to fight about who was in control of her body. But the case of John, a case that I believe meets the diagnostic criteria for a major depressive disorder, is a different matter. I feel that this patient is not able to take responsibility for his living. I think we have to do it for him awhile.

Q: One of the things I want to comment on is that there is a certain transparency about this case; it is very easy to achieve a ready consensus or a consensual validity about what is going on and what should be done. But what about when you eventually have to deal with the patient getting better? Maybe taking the gun back is a sign of his health, not of rescue fantasies or of coercion. Shouldn't we try to transcend what is presented to us and ask "what if?" What's missing? What do we need to know to, perhaps, make some other interpretations and not readily arrive at foregone conclusions?

A (Heilig): I think that is a very important comment. I think the gun issue is subsidiary to the therapy issue: What do you do with a high-risk suicidal man who wants to drop out of therapy? I think that is the primary issue in this case. The gun is a red herring in a sense. It is interesting but I think the important thing is to maintain some therapeutic connection here. My own approach would be to explore what the family might offer and to see that the therapeutic plan is in place, not to let this guy just slip through the cracks.

A (Yufit): I would agree. I think we have a group countertransference here. All of us need closure to make ourselves feel more comfortable in a situation like this, and I think we can do that prematurely.

A (Maltsberger): Do we ever have any right at all, morally or otherwise, to interfere with someone who is committing suicide? My view is yes, we do. Why? Well, one good practical answer, among several possibilities, is that the great majority of suicidal patients who recover from their depressive episodes are glad to find themselves still alive. So I think that we have an ethical/moral obligation to buy them some time.

A (Heilig): I think there is more than just an ethical/moral issue here, and that is the issue of malpractice. If you do not respond when somebody comes to you in a suicidal crisis, you are exposed to the possible risk of a malpractice claim.

Q: I think we do have evidence that the therapist, from fairly early on, was caught off-balance. There is a power struggle going on even before the gun is referenced in this case. The therapist suggested hospitalization and medications to the patient, and the patient declined. I would have been very interested in doing what I believe Mr. Heilig suggested, a very thorough examination of what John's understanding of his problems were and why he was coming into therapy at this point, rather than taking the obvious precipitant breakup as his reason for entering treatment. What is suggested to me is that this man has a rejecting family. Dr. Maltsberger has pointed out that the family has very little emotional interest in the patient. He has just been or at least has felt rejected by his girl friend. If, as is suggested, he has just gone off of cocaine, I think he experienced even a third loss at that point. What is happening now in the therapy is that he is precipitating the rejection of the therapist as well. So one of the things I would have been inclined to do differently would have been to enter into the issue of loss. As the situation escalated, as it most certainly would have, I would not have focused so much on the gun itself as on the metaphor behind it; that is, his wish to have me, also, give him the means to break this relationship, for me to give him permission to kill himself—to reject him. I would have been curious about why, after having gone through so many rejections, he had the need to repeat this with me.

What the therapist apparently did was to directly counter his resistance. We know that when you do that with an agitated patient, you are going to get increased resistance. There would have been ways, I am sure, to have tried to side with some of that resistance, saying, "Yes, I understand your wanting the gun, in part. But what occurs to me is that you may be willing to end your life at this point, before you have given us a chance to really understand you and work. I am curious about that. Teach me more about that. Let's explore more about that." You have not at that point

said, "No, I am not going to give you your gun." Instead, you, have joined
with him, and you might see where that goes. Nothing is foolproof, but
I think that point would have given him more of an opportunity to see
what he wanted to do, and it would have given him the opportunity to
work more on maintaining the alliance with the therapist.

A (Heilig): Clearly, we have inadequate information about the dynamics
of this man, but I see the gun as symbolic of the patient's strenuous
effort to make a connection. This is a guy who has suffered a lot of
disappointments and loss. I think there was probably not much of a
relationship with his family. Certainly, there was a lot of denial regarding his earlier suicide attempt and probably of other problems he
has experienced: he didn't make it in medical school, he just lost a girl
friend, and he has never lived up to his own expectations or, most
likely, those of his family. No, I think his effort to align himself very
tightly with a therapist scares him. At the beginning, he is not sure he
can trust this relationship. I think giving the gun has a lot of symbolic
meaning to him, about giving to a therapist what guns symbolize. He
is handing over his power in a sense. I think he is getting scared, and
that is why he wants to withdraw and also that he is testing this therapist
to see how vigorous he is going to be in staying in this relationship
with him.

A (Yufit): There is one positive point in John's therapy that I think we are
overlooking. John was "initially cooperative" in therapy. What happened
there? Why was he initially cooperative? I think understanding this factor
gives some hope, perhaps, that we could engage John in other struggles
and by doing so, buy the time so many of us feel is important.

Q: I think most of us who are not inclined to encourage patients to give
us their guns would nevertheless take the gun if it was brought to us more
spontaneously than it was in this case. I am particularly interested to hear
more about Mr. Heilig's thinking. You are someone who regularly encourages people to bring the gun in. Why do you take that tactic, and why
do you think it works?

A (Heilig): I do not do it in all cases, but if I consider the case acutely
suicidal and dangerous, where there is a suicidal implement in place, I
think it is useful to get rid of lethal materials.

Q: In particular, I wonder why you choose to have it brought to you,
rather than to have evidence brought to you that it has been disposed of
otherwise.

A (Heilig): Well, I think it is an indication of trust. It is a demonstration
of my active intervention. I mean to intrude here and do something about

the possibility of suicide. It bonds us (my patient and I) in a certain way. There are some situations in which I wouldn't want to do this at all. I would be very careful about psychotic people, for example. I would want to maintain a very careful kind of relationship until I had more evidence as to what to expect.

Comment: Some very simple summary points. First, it is very difficult to teach therapists to ask and to do something about an available weapon such as a gun. Additionally, it is difficult to teach therapists to negotiate with patients, for example, to put the gun in a safe deposit box so that it could not be dealt with impulsively. Also, we as therapists often do not know what the law is in the community about weapons possession. The bottom line is the theme of these case presentations—prevention. Ultimately, the gun is an element, one element, of transaction within the therapeutic relationship wherein one goal is to ensure the patient's safety and to negotiate a shared goal for a more fulfilled and meaningful life.

REFERENCES

Farberow, N. L., Shneidman, E. S., & Neuringer, C. (1970). Case history and neuropsychiatric hospitalization factors in suicide. In E. S. Shneidman, N. L. Farberow, & R. E. Litman (Eds.), *The psychology of suicide* (pp. 385–402). New York: Science House.

Richman, J. (1971). Family determinants of suicide potential. In D. Anderson & L. J. McClain (Eds.), *Identifying suicidal potential* (pp. 33–54). New York: Behavioral Publications.

Sabbath, J. C. (1969). The suicidal adolescent—the expendable child. *Journal of the American Academy of Child Psychiatry, 8,* 272–289.

Tarasoff v. Regents of University of California, 529 P2d 553 (Cal. 1974); 551 P2d 334 (Cal. 1976).

Virkunnen, M. (1976). Attitude to psychiatric treatment before suicide in schizophrenia and paranoid psychoses. *British Journal of Psychiatry, 128,* 47–49.

6

Malpractice

Traditionally, society has assigned blame for every death. Natural and accidental deaths occur by God's will; homicides and suicides are due to man's interventions. Where man was to blame, the guilty had to be punished. With regard to suicide, when punishments were first instituted, they were based on religious, political, practical, or economic grounds. For example, in early Roman law, deterrent sanctions against suicide were applied only to criminals, soldiers, and slaves.

It was not sufficient that the death of the suicide had already occurred. In early Athens it was customary to chop off the hand of the suicide, preferably that with which he had taken his life. For centuries, English law called for more severe punishments: the cadaver was subject to a variety of indignities and degradations, sanctions were placed on the manner and place of burial, and property was confiscated.

By the early 19th century, however, social attitudes moderated, and suicide increasingly became considered a deviation from normality, a subject for medical and social investigation. The last of the English penal statutes against suicide was repealed in 1961. In the United States, the decriminalization of suicide is now unanimous, although about one half of the states still consider it a felony to aid, abet, or encourage a suicide. Judicial attitudes toward suicide have shifted from focusing on the guilt and punshiment of the suicide to protecting suicidal persons from themselves (i.e., preventing suicide) and recognizing the pain and suffering of survivors left bereft of the variety of roles played by their suicided relative.

Suicide implicitly points a finger of blame at those involved in the life of the decedent, covertly—and sometimes overtly—making survivors feel responsible for the death itself, for not rescuing the decedent or preventing the suicide, or for not making life more tolerable so that the suicide need not have occurred. It should come as no surpise that if there is *someone else* to blame, there will be a tendency to displace and externalize that felt blame.

Therapists are uniquely positioned to be targets of that blame as about one in every six completed suicides was in some form of treatment at the time of their suicide. Two recent national surveys (Chemtob, Hamada, Bauer, Kinney, & Torigoe, 1988; Chemtob, Hamada, Bauer, Torigoe, & Kinney, 1988) found that 51% of psychiatrists and 22% of psychologists have experienced a patient's suicide, with 55% and 39%, respectively, having lost a second patient to suicide.

Thus, the treatment of the suicidal patient brings with it an accompanying risk for the suicide of that patient and the subsequent possibility of legal action brought against the therapist by grieving survivors. If the patient was entrusted to the care of a therapist, the patient's death now implicitly points a finger of blame at that therapist for failing to provide adequate care.

The helper-patient relationship places certain role obligations on the helper. These may be best summarized as a responsibility to do "everything possible" to protect the health of the patient. With respect to suicide, this essentially means that therapists are expected to prevent suicide if suicide prevention can be done reasonably.

The courts increasingly have come to an enlightened understanding of what is *reasonable*. This represents an acknowledgment of today's trend toward less restrictive care and maximization of patient responsibilities. Judgments of liability are supposed to be based on evidence of a breach of a specific duty of care, by some act of omission or commission, that is judged to be proximally causative of the patient's suicide. The duty of care is judged relative to what would be expected of the reasonable and prudent practitioner. The reader may note that these words and phrases appear to lack operational specificity. It is for this reason that the courts rely on expert testimony to help determine whether a therapist's actions constitute a breach in the expected standard of care. However, even where such testimony exonerates the therapist, juries may disagree and award significant monetary compensation to survivor plaintiffs (cf., Goldstein, 1987).

As one example of the frequency with which malpractice actions are initiated against therapists, the American Psychological Association's Insurance Trust reported, as of May 31, 1988, that patient suicides accounted for approximately 6% of all malpractice claims brought against psychologists but 11% of all liability insurance payouts (Pope, 1989). The frequency of claims has increased dramatically in more recent years, reflecting an increasingly litigious trend in society (Berman, 1986), although only a small proportion of these claims get to court and a possible jury verdict.

Psychiatrists, even more than psychologists, are likely targets of malpractice actions because of their relatively more frequent inpatient practices and their use of potentially abused medications in treatment of suicidal patients. The following case, that of a suit against a psychiatrist alleging malpractice in the treatment of a psychiatrist-patient who suicided, is somewhat atypical of these cases. However, it does highlight well for the therapist-reader the need for attention to good treatment. To that end, the reader is directed to two published guidelines; Berman and Cohen-Sandler (1983) and Pope (1986), that recommend a variety of strategies for meeting adequate standards of care in the treatment of suicidal patients.

Of all methods of suicide prevention available to the practicing clinician, the early detection of risk and the effective treatment of the at-risk patient perhaps best fit the training and skills of the mental health practitioner. Consideration of these guidelines in the context of the consultations provided in response to this case by the panel of experts potentially raises the standard of care to a more optimal level than most practitioners currently provide. It is with that goal in mind that malpractice cases may serve both as powerful teachers and as spurs for the development of more effective suicide prevention efforts.

CASE STUDY: MARY

Mary, a 34-year-old, married psychiatrist, sought outpatient psychotherapy from a consultant to her inpatient service (Dr. Smith). Presenting problems included intense fearfulness, low self-esteem, and chronic depression, for which she had had two prior therapists. Over the subsequent 2 years, Mary was seen by Dr. Smith in individual group and/or marital therapy (with combinations of two of these three modalities concurrent at any one time). During this time Mary also entered and became a member of Dr. Smith's "counter transference supervision group" with several other mental health professionals as co-members.

The oldest child of two physicians, Mary had been an exceptional student (4.0 GPA in college) but lived in constant fear of losing her father's love should she fail to meet perceived performance expectations. In this vein, she saw her father as all-controlling. Her presenting symptoms, including frequent protestations of hopelessness, were related to these fears of failure and loss of love.

Toward the end of the second year of treatment, several events occurred within a short time. Mary gave birth to her first child; she bought and moved into a new house, taking on a sizable mortgage; and she opened a part-time solo private practice. Under pressure of these events, she became increasingly depressed, moody, obsessional, and frequently angry. A threatened staff reduction at the hospital caused her great worry, which led her, in turn, to cancel several of her private patient hours. Because of these cancellations she further worried that she would be sued, lose income, be unable to carry her new mortgage, and so on. When her supervisor at the hospital recommended that she reduce pressure and anxiety by cutting back her work hours, she interpreted this as evidence of her failure, and her anxiety exacerbated.

Soon thereafter, Mary became increasingly suicidal. When found by her husband to be sitting, staring vacantly, and holding a vial of pills in her hand, she was brought to a local psychiatric hospital and admitted for 72-hour observation. In the hospital Mary was cooperative with all procedures. She claimed that her suicidal behavior had been both "hysterical" and designed to express her rage at her artist-husband for not supporting her better. She was released to the care of Dr. Smith (discharge diagnosis: Obsessive-Compulsive Personality Disorder with Hysterical Features) with discharge prescriptions for Haldol,® Deseryl,® Cogentin,® and Sinequan.® However, Dr. Smith strongly recommended that Mary go off all medication ("drugs are an artificial crutch") and angrily chided her for her manipulative and childlike behavior. He told Mary to "stop being a wimp" and suggested to her that "maybe she didn't have what it took to be a good therapist." He dismissed Mary's suicidality as "wholly manipulative." Within 6 weeks Mary's anxiety and agitation worsened. She had lost 8 pounds, was sleeping only fitfully, and spoke often of her hopelessness and helplessness. When she refused to go to her therapy group, her husband angrily walked out with their child. When he returned the next morning, he found her still in bed. Unable to reach Dr. Smith by phone, he called her superior at the hospital, who came to the house, evaluated her as in need of immediate hospitalization, and arranged for a voluntary admission. On intake Mary was described as guarded, evasive, anxious, and agitated, expressing feelings of worthlessness and guilt with suicide ideation. Her condition was diagnosed as a Major Depression, and she was placed on suicide precautions.

Dr. Smith never did return Mary's husband's phone call and learned of her hospitalization only through the grapevine. During this hospitalization, Dr. Smith made no in-person contact with Mary but did have two telephone consultations. Mary's in-hospital therapist, Dr. Jones, called Dr. Smith to express "great concern about boundary violations," but Dr. Smith did not see these as at all "dangerous." As Mary's condition improved, suicide precautions were discontinued and a weekend pass with her husband was ordered. Plans for discharge were discussed on stipulation that

Mary end her participation in Dr. Smith's supervision group, thereby working with Dr. Smith only in therapist-patient contracts. A decision as to whether Mary wanted to continue working with Dr. Smith in individual and marital therapy was left for further discussion among Mary, her husband, and Dr. Smith.

Two weeks after her admission, Mary was discharged to the care of Dr. Smith. Two days after her release from the hospital, on the eve of her first postdischarge session with Dr. Smith, Mary's child cried incessantly and was brought into bed with Mary and her husband. When her husband awoke in the morning, Mary was not in bed. He found her several minutes later on the bathroom floor. Cause of death was acute barbiturate intoxication due to ingestion of overdose.

Suit is brought by Mary's husband against Dr. Smith for malpractice, and his therapy notes are subpoenaed. Upon examination, they contain copies of treatment bills and a summary note written from recall 2 months after Mary's suicide. In this summary, Dr. Smith simply states that he did not consider Mary to be suicidal.

The presenting issue is to offer your opinion regarding Dr. Smith's treatment of Mary and the hospital's treatment and discharge planning, relative to the charge of malpractice. If asked, would you agree to testify for the plaintiff or the defendant, and why?

COMMENTARY

Seymour Perlin:

The case of Mary invites us to review many "management" issues in the evaluation, hospital treatment, and outpatient care of the suicidal patient. The picture provided also demands due consideration of caregiver attitudes to suicidal behavior.

Mary, a physician, has had episodes of depression for which she sought help from two prior therapists, apparently without help or any current alliance. We note the history of a sense of failure or fear of failure in the context of success. Chronic depression is noteworthy, as is her response to increased stress and concomitant anxiety. Such symptoms may indeed lead to behaviors that provide substance to her feared and anticipated failure. Anger and obsessions, as well as suicidality, mean that we must consider a major depression and a personality disorder and must also rule out other diagnoses (including substance abuse). There are implications of a psychosocial crisis reflecting interpersonal conflict with her artist-husband, whom she perceives as unsupportive, perhaps fulfilling the expected loss of love from male figures. Notwithstanding the multiple modalities of therapy, a crisis situation develops resulting in hospitalization. The questionable polypharmacy of multiple medications seems to be directed at underlying conditions beyond the discharge diagnosis; the use of two antidepressants would raise questions about what is being treated. Indeed, at the time of hospitalization she seemed confused and near-delusional in her self-evaluation. Postpartum considerations are not delineated.

Following discharge, Mary becomes increasingly suicidal. Medication issues are not addressed; there is a window of vulnerability in terms of partial response and access to pills (an issue posed particularly by the physican-patient). There is no mention of side effects of the medication and how such signs as dystonia are experienced by the patient. (There is no mention of consideration of alternate medications, e.g., a different class of antidepressants to which the patient might be more reponsive.) On the one hand, we need to know whether the medication was adequate—that is, whether the multiple medications were appropriate and of adequate dosage and duration; on the other hand, we should not assume a priori that the medication was taken at all. Needless to say, we must also note that Mary is responded to negatively by a "punitive" therapist who recommends that she should "go off all medication."

Following her readmission, improvement presumably occurred but perhaps only enough to carry out her plan to escape from pain. The diagnosis at the time of rehospitalization was a major depression, but there is no information as to whether medication was prescribed at all and if so, whether it was appropriately prescribed. We need to know, as well, any history of untoward responses to her crying child, for example, feelings that she might harm the child and/or feel unable to attend to the child's needs. That is an area of history that certainly should be elaborated.

The notes indicate that there has been an inadequate diagnostic evaluation, inadequate assessment of her mental status, inadequate assessment of suicidality, a lack of adequate and considered use of medication, a failure to consider alternative medication to which the patient might be more responsive, and a lack of adequate or considered psychotherapy. There appears to have been a lack of adequate or considered suicidal precaution, for example, the presence of medications available in the home (how large a prescription was provided, to whom was the prescription given, who had the pills, etc.?). There was a lack of adequate or considered discharge planning. Discharge planning is an essential issue in review of these cases. Clearly, there was a lack of adequate or considered involvement of the family in discharge planning.

With regard to the therapist, he was unavailable as needed, did not work out a response or treatment plan of any kind, and did not take charge of the case. Finally, the therapist did not adequately document whatever was done in the way of assessment or care.

Ronald Maris:

Before I respond to the specific questions we were given to answer, let me mention a few considerations as a prologue. Of course, I understand and accept the limitations with which we must work in addressing this case; namely a 1½ page statement of Mary's case. The reader must understand that this is a totally inadequate data base for the mandate which we have. The only appropriate response to express regarding this case, given the limited data base, is that no responsible opinion can be rendered. When in real life I am asked to consult on such cases, I obviously would receive and be privy to much more data: complete hospital records, depositions by all key parties involved in the suit, often my own interviews, site visits, psychological testing, a complete history and chronology of the case, key actors in the issues, the depositions of other experts, letters, diaries, news accounts, and so on. I think this is important to note because, after all, we want to be fair to all sides in these issues.

In that vein this is a highly biased case presentation, sympathetic to the plaintiff and very hostile toward Dr. Smith and, to a lesser degree, toward the hospital. Dr. Smith may deserve it, but I have my doubts that his case has been fairly presented. We need more information about Mary's chronic depression, for which she had seen two prior therapists. There are many questions that should be raised about those previous therapies. How long had she been depressed? What were her previous diagnoses? Where are the notes from her previous therapies? How long was she treated? How long had she been on which medications, if any?

For many of the social and epidemiological factors to which we might attend, Mary was a low suicide risk. Obviously, she is young, a married woman with a child, was quite bright, got good grades in school and university, and was a medical professional. Psychiatric help was readily available, she had some insight into her problems, her parents were physicians, and so on. Did she really have a 4.0 grade point average? Usually the truth is something more like 3.92 or 3.88. I think that is a very significant question to ask because if, in fact, her GPA was not 4.0, then her need to maintain perfection has already been compromised, and her dynamics are quite different. If it indeed is 4.0, then I'm reminded of Smith's concept of ego-vulnerability (Smith, 1985), of high-expectations. If it is not, then I think in some way the pressure is off already.

Obviously, there are many recent changes in her life, including the birth of a first child, a new mortgage, and the opening of a private practice.

These changes should remind us that thresholds of adaptation can be breached in anyone. Even if these changes are experienced as particularly positive, I think of Holmes and Rahe's (1967) work on stress and life crises in which positive experiences, like getting married and taking on a mortgage, are considered very stressful. One can quantify and evaluate the multiplicative impact of these factors. The threatened staff reduction should sensitize us to social disorganization factors contributing to personal disorganization. I am reminded of a book I read as a suicidology fellow at The Johns Hopkins Medical School, Kobler and Stotland's *The End of Hope* (1964) and of a study by Rose Coser (1976) called "Suicide and the Relational System," which suggest that social disorganization is often related to personal disorganization. We often tend to overlook this relationship.

In my reading of the case, the mention of Haldol comes out of the blue. For the first time we learn that Mary is more than simply depressed, that there are psychotic or major anxiety issues in the case. The fact that she is sleeping fitfully probably is significant. None of these predictors are separate factors to be considered in isolation. In a study of suicide in Chicago (Maris, 1981), terminal insomnia—waking up early and being unable to go back to sleep—was highly predictive of completed suicides but not of control subjects (nonfatal suicide attempters and natural deaths).

Dr. Smith is a disaster! He (she?) seems too bad to be true and therefore I am suspicious. Dr. Litman says that fact is often stranger than fiction, so maybe this therapist is for real. We are also encouraged to think about what is now general knowledge about hospitalized depressed patients: when they improve, one has to be very careful about removing suicidal precautions, giving weekend passes, and so on.

Let me now turn quickly to the several questions I was asked to address. What about Dr. Smith's treatment? Superficially, this is a too obvious case of malpractice. We know that Dr. Smith saw Mary for about 2 years in a combination of individual, group, and marital therapies. We do not know what the treatment was. What was his DSM-III or DSM-III-R diagnosis? Were any medications prescribed? What was his treatment plan? In retrospect, we simply learn that no progress testing was performed. There were, in the file after the death, a summary note written 2 months after Mary's suicide and a few copies of bills. That was all that was in her file. So maybe there was not anything to report. We do know, too, that Dr. Smith did not even see Mary for her second hospitalization for a major depression and suicidal ideation and perhaps not for the first hospitalization. Nor did he return Mary's husband's phone call.

It is unusual for a competent psychiatrist to say some of the things that were allegedly said by Dr. Smith. His comments seem to be made without reflection; remarks like "manipulative wimp" and "drugs are a crutch." If it is being accurately reported, this case is altogether a clear case of malpractice by Dr. Smith.

What about the hospital treatment? There were two hospitalizations that we know about. Presumably, Mary's husband brought her in for 72-hour observation because she was suicidal. It is not clear who treated her at the hospital. Dr. Smith is not mentioned except in regard to Mary's being discharged to him. The first hospital diagnosis is in an Axis-II code: Obsessive-Compulsive Personality Disorder with Hysterical Features. For this problem, we hear only of medications being given—namely, Haldol, Cogentin, Sinquan, and Deseryl—again implying that Mary may have a psychotic disorder or extreme agitation. Six weeks later Mary is back in the hospital with a major depressive disorder and more suicidal ideation. A Dr. Jones treated her for 2 weeks. We are not told what the treatment was, just that Mary improved and was discharged to Dr. Smith. What about the hospital's discharge planning? Clearly discharging a patient to Dr. Smith, given all we know now, is highly questionable. He did not come to the hospital in person to see Mary, he did not support her drug therapy; he did not help her much after the first hospitalization. Interestingly, we note that Mary suicided on the eve of her first visit to Dr. Smith after leaving the hospital.

The home situation was not supportive. She had a small child and a husband with whom she was extremely angry. Obviously, with depression, many of Mary's problems are not resolvable in just 2 weeks of hospital treatment.

Would I testify for the plaintiff or the defendent? The answer is for the plaintiff. However, as I have noted, I am not convinced that Dr. Smith's or the hospital's version of Mary's illness and treatment have been fully presented to us. I think it is extremely important that we not caricature this case. No one has taken the hospital's or Dr. Smith's position and described it in any detail at all.

Robert Litman:

John Mack (1988), viewing the threat of nuclear war as suicide, has observed that young men are socialized to be competitive and trained to enter society prepared for battle. If you are called on to be an expert witness in a malpractice case, you might well feel that you are preparing to participate in a battle. Usually, the principals in a malpractice case have very deep antagonistic feelings. In this case there is a husband, a widower raising an orphan child, who feels extremely bitter toward the doctor and the hospital. The doctor, on the other hand, feels that he has been unjustly tricked by fate, and he is defensive, probably also hurt and angry.

Each side is championed by an attorney or a team of attorneys who are trained to battle in court for money. The attorneys call on experts, in this case suicidologists, to act as staff persons, to interpret events, to answer their questions, and to give them advice.

The rules permit these attorneys to discover in advance what opposing experts will say in court. The two sides evaluate each other's strengths and weaknesses. Then, usually, such cases are settled by negotiation. The reasons for settlement are persuasive and are similar to the reasons a negotiated peace is usually preferable to an all-out war. Of the more than 100 malpractice cases I have reviewed for attorneys, fewer than 10 have actually gone to trial.

I charge a retainer fee in advance to review plaintiffs' cases because often the allegations of professional negligence or malpractice have no merit. If that is the case, I tell the lawyers, "Forget it, you don't have a case in my opinion." I often then meet with the grieving and angry family to do bereavement counseling. Frequently, however, I will say to the attorney, "Go ahead, it looks like you have reasonable grounds for a lawsuit, at least you will discover more clearly what actually happened."

Similarly, when I consult with the defense, I may tell the attorneys that there was obvious negligence here and that they should settle the case as quickly as possible; or on the contrary, I may say that the case should be defended because there was no malpractice. To make these decisions, the expert witness reviews, as a minimum, the records of the coroner and of the police and the various records of the doctors and the hospitals. As the case develops, various statements made under oath (depositions) will be received. Finally, each side will be prepared with its own version of the facts and its own interpretation of what happened. Both sides will be ready to argue these views in court in an adversarial contest.

Turning to the protocol of concern here, I note that it is incomplete and biased and thus pretty typical of what I might get originally from a plaintiff's attorney. The attorney would read this to me on the telephone or send it to me in a letter, observing, "This is our version of the case. What do you think?" I might say of this case, "To the extent that these allegations are factual, you seem to have a pretty good case. Do I understand that you intend to bring suit against not only the doctor primarily involved but also the hospital and all of the other doctors too?"

I would expect the attorney to subpoena everybody's records, their process notes, payment records, and correspondence. From the plaintiff's point of view, the absence of notes by Dr. Smith is extremely damaging to him. I would suggest to the plaintiff's attorney that as soon as possible he should send interrogatories to Dr. Smith. These are demands for answers to questions, for example, concerning Smith's general practice with regard to notes. The plaintiff's attorney wants to find out as soon as possible Dr. Smith's attitudes and practices about note taking and about prescribing antidepressant drugs. If he replies that he never uses antidepressants and he never takes notes, he should not be treating depressed or suicidal people, even though he may be a talented psychotherapist. Then it would look even more as if the plaintiff has a good case. If, in fact, the doctor's standard practice with depressed and suicidal patients is to give antidepressant drugs and to take notes, then he has a lot of explaining to do about his treatment of Mary.

It is very difficult to defend a malpractice case when the doctor has no notes. In this case the husband will take the witness stand and say, "Dr. Smith insulted my wife, and he made her condition worse. He said many things to her that hurt her feelings and lowered her self-esteem." If Dr. Smith remembers the events differently, he will have a hard time persuading the jury that his memory is better than the husband's. After all, Dr. Smith has lots of patients, at least 20 a year, maybe 50 or more. Mary's husband has only this one case to keep in mind, so his memory of what happened is probably more accurate than that of Dr. Smith. The husband is going to say that Dr. Smith told him, "The suicidal behaviors of Mary are just manipulations and they don't really count. She is just putting on an act. Don't take it seriously. If she gives you too much trouble, walk out. That is why I walked out." In retrospect, that advice by Dr. Smith seems like very bad advice. Without notes, can Dr. Smith explain himself?

But this case report is highly biased for the plaintiff. It is really interesting to consider what I would say if the defense had asked me to consult. Then I would review in my mind the definition of malpractice. Dr. Smith is required to behave toward his patient, Mary, according to the standard of a reasonably prudent and competent psychiatrist under the same conditions. I would need to undertake a special kind of psychological autopsy, focusing not on the feelings of the deceased but on the performance and the actions of the doctor, the hosptial, and the entire staff.

For hospitals the standard of care is comparatively clear. The hospital accreditation committee of the American Association of Suicidology has been evaluating hospital standards for a long time. By now each hospital has in writing its own policies and standards for the care of potentially suicidal patients.

However, doctors in the private practice of outpatient psychiatry do not have written standards. In each case the issue of the doctor's performance, whether it was competent and prudent, eventually is evaluated by a court after hearing testimony from experts and arguments from attorneys. The jury will evaluate the credibility of each witness and make a judgment on the facts. Juries reach decisions on the basis of common sense and, of course, some prejudice.

Prejudice is an interesting sidelight to every case. In this case the jury is likely to have prejudice in favor of the widower and his orphan child. But wait a minute. Suppose it emerges that this husband had been having an extramarital love affair while Mary was suicidal! Then the prejudice would swing in the other direction.

Would I be a consultant for the defense? Of course! Suppose the defense attorney sent me this protocol and said, "I haven't got all the records and the statements together yet because the plaintiff has just recently filed suit, but these are the allegations by the other side. What do you think?" I would tell the attorney that if these allegations are true after all the facts are in, then the defense will want to settle this case and offer the full extent of Dr. Smith's insurance. Plaintiff's attorneys are usually willing to accept such an offer. The reason they will accept the offer is that no one can know for sure when they go to trial just how a jury will decide the case.

I would say to the attorney, "Immediately, you must have a long talk with Dr. Smith. Have him look at this protocol and then dictate or write out or type a complete answer, his version of the facts. Ask him to give you five reasons why he thought Mary was not suicidal. Have him give you three reasons why he thought drug treatment was not indicated and three reasons why he did not keep notes." Suppose he tells his attorney that, of course, he keeps notes in all cases, but he made an exception in this one. It was a special exception because Mary ordered him to keep no notes. She said that because she was a psychiatrist, "I don't want this to go on my record." She said, "If you keep notes, I won't come and talk with you." Suppose Dr. Smith tells his attorney, "I give antidepressant drugs all the time to depressed patients. But again, this was a special case. I evaluated Mary carefully and repeatedly, and in her case the Haldol, Desyrel, and all the other drugs she had been taking were causing more harm than they were helping. I thought this over very carefully before I recommended that she stop taking drugs." With this type of information Dr. Smith starts to develop a position that can be defended.

Suppose Dr. Smith lists all of the reasons he felt that Mary would not commit suicide. He lists various sociological factors [as described by Dr. Maris (1987)] and explains why, in Mary's case, he did not think there would be a postpartum depression. It is possible that Mary told Dr. Smith many times that she was never going to kill herself.

At some time before the settlement conference I would want to talk with Dr. Smith myself. What kind of a person is this doctor? Is he really paternalistic and punitive? If he is in fact cold, autocratic, and defensive, I would tell the lawyer to settle this case as soon as possible and not let it go any further. But suppose Dr. Smith turns out to be a really nice guy, or in fact a truly great psychiatrist, a renaissance man. After all, Dr. Smith did consult with Mary for 2 years. Who would know her better than this doctor? And it was Mary's choice to see Dr. Smith. She persisted in seeing Dr. Smith when she could have gone to anybody. She must have had some good reasons for choosing him. And so on. There are two sides to every case. The role of the expert witness in court is quite different from the role of the principals and of the attorneys. They are the fighters, the adversaries. The expert is there to inform the jury and the judge and to provide material to assist them in making their judgments; and the opinions of the expert must be backed by reasonable facts and reasonable past experiences. Although the expert has a certain point of view that is favorable to the position of the attorney who has called him into court (otherwise the expert would not be there), the expert should keep in mind that there are two sides to every case (otherwise it wouldn't get as far as a trial). So the expert should resist any temptation to go to extremes to win points for a particular attorney. As a judge once admonished me when I became overly sharp in defending myself against a rather strenuous cross-examination, "Those two lawyers—they are the adversaries. They are the people who are having the contest. You and I are just here to inform the jury."

Questions and Responses

Comment (Perlin): Just one point about standards of care. In some of the cases I have seen recently, the standard of care would be, by most frames of reference, "reasonable." But if it is not, the standard of care is defined by the by-laws of the hospital or the psychiatric unit. It is very important to recognize that the unit's by-laws legitimize standards of practice on that unit. If the by-laws for the nursing staff say, for example, "All patients in suicidal precautions must be checked every 15 minutes" that is the by-law that must be carried out. In many instances, the hospital or the nursing staff put this into the record as their standard of care, but then very few staff are trained to know what these by-laws are. So I think you have to know both *reasonable* generic standard of care and also the standards of care as explicitly stated in the by-laws of the organization (the ward unit, the hospital, etc.) with which you are associated. In most of the reviews I have done, the staff did not know their own by-laws.

Comment (Maris): I would just like to emphasize what Dr. Litman has said. The issue of what *really* happened in these cases is often a very critical one. You have to be very careful, take the seemingly implausible defense side, and try to see how you might be able to support the defense. The procedure is much like a journal article. When somebody writes and publishes a paper, somebody else then criticizes the paper, and somebody writes a rebuttal. If you stop with the criticism, you may think, this is obviously clear and correct. Then you read the rebuttal and you think, "No, something else probably is correct." It is very important not to stop just with what you are given. I find that in most legal cases I can make an argument for either side. Over the years I have become more and more like the lawyers, leaving final decisions to the jury. There are, of course, some cases in which it is transparently obvious that one side has no case. I will drop out in such cases if I believe I am on the wrong side. But many times it is certainly not clear initially what really happened.

Q: Were Dr. Smith a psychologist there is what appears to me to be a clear ethical violation (there is, I believe, more than one) that no one really mentioned. It is what is known as a "dual relationship." Dr. Smith played both therapist *and* supervisor, exercising an inordinate amount of potential control over this patient/supervisee that is essentially frowned on by the profession. Embedded in that is the question, is an ethics violation, ipso facto, malpractice?

As a related question, if we can assume that some of the comments attributed to Dr. Smith—for example, the comment about being a "wimp," which might be seen as pejorative, punitive, and so on—might be described by Dr. Smith as, first, taken entirely out of context and, second, as fitting his general style of being a confrontational therapist—that is, the way he motivates as a therapist—we might merely say that he has a style we frown on. On the one hand, I assume we could make a case that there are confrontational therapists who do good work. On the other hand, at what point does that style perhaps border on expressing a contemptuous attitude; and does a contemptuous attitude toward one's patient constitute grounds for malpractice?

A (Litman): The first question relates to the confusion of roles or "boundary violations," as Dr. Jones put it. Yes, there were. Those psychiatrists who as a rule do not use drugs and feel that drugs are just a crutch would be practicing on a modified analytical or some sort of personal psychotherapy model. They would have it in mind, probably, that they would be crossing ethical boundaries if they confused authority roles as a consultant and leader of psychotherapy supervision group, ongoing at the same time as they participated in psychotherapy with the doctor as a patient. However, on the other side is the idea that this is a chronic case. It has been going on for a couple of years. It is a difficult case. In such a chronic and difficult case there is a temptation—and maybe it can be justified—to put all of the authority and therapy roles together, to be a real person, participating in a confrontational way with the patient's life. At least that is what Dr. Smith might say.

A (Perlin): We should be aware of the fact that there are very eminent therapists who are testifying that unless a *particular* form of therapy is used, one that has been scientifically evaluted—for example, cognitive and interpersonal therapy—that an *appropriate* therapy designed to treat the depressed patient was not utilized; and therefore the patient was deprived of the benefit of that therapy. This position, if adopted as a standard at any given time, freezes the development of or experimentation in new therapies that might be even more appropriate. If you know that Dr. X is going to testify for the opposing side in that way, then that becomes a pressure that moves settlement in certain directions as well. I think it is a very important issue when major figures in the field begin to adopt a particular stance.

Comment (from audience): I wish somebody had approached me and said, "Would you be willing to consult in this case?" because, as Dr. Maris and the others have pointed out, it sounds so terrible that it would be an opportunity to consult on the side of the plaintiff. In my experience almost every case that has been brought to me has been a more or less frivolous attempt on the part of the plaintiff to generate compensation. In my own experience, when an attorney asks me, "In what proportion of cases have you testified for the defense and for the plaintiff?" I answer that I don't have any plaintiff case. So I would welcome this case as a great opportunity to have one plaintiff case on my list of experiences. However, I am not quite as ready as Dr. Litman to say, "Of course, I would take this case." If I were called by the defense, and this was all the data available, and it was all verified by documentation, I'd say, "I would not want to testify in this case. I do not think there is any defense. So you better settle if you can."

There are a couple of things that intrigue me. No one pursued the possibility that Dr. Smith might be a woman. Many female patients prefer female therapists, and we might change our positions slightly if we see Dr. Smith as a woman.

The standard of care is an area for tremendous disagreement among experienced clinicians. I don't think there is an *established* standard of care beyond, as Dr. Litman pointed out in his latter comments, documenting the rationale for what you do. If you do something atypical and if you document why you are doing it, for example, "this is an atypical treatment but under such and such circumstances I feel that this is the appropriate thing to do at this time, for this patient," I would say you are within the standard of care. I am working on a case now in which the physician gave a seriously, chronically depressed, suicidal patient "box flour powder treatment," acupuncture, psychic, and meditation. The physician—a woman—is being sued because of these unusual treatment modalities. The more chronic the case, and therefore the better we know the patient, the further we tend to get from "traditional" methods of treatment. That traditional treatments have not been effective may be a strong argument for the nontraditional. If I read this case correctly, we have a chronic problem, a characterological problem. This is not just an illness that occurred and then was going to get better with standard approaches. If traditional treatments had worked, this patient would not have been suicidal. It is often possible, I think, to defend, to explain to a jury, that ordinary treatment, a so-called standard of care, really has not helped the patient. That is why various things were tried.

Dr. Maris referred to this patient as having low-risk characteristics. I don't see that at all. This patient is a woman physician with characterological difficulties, uncertainties, and low self-esteem, whose marriage is not that solid, whose practice is gradually deteriorating, whose self-esteem is going down the tubes, and who is not responding to traditional therapy. She is a very high-risk. Her high level of education; high intelligence; adequate financial resources; and the fact that she is a professional person—all of these place her in the high-risk category. Her husband is apparently not supportive; she has chronic difficulties and two prior therapies. We have empirical data that two or more prior attempts to get help that were not successful puts one in a high-risk category. So I would evaluate this is as a very high-risk.

With regard to the standard of care in an institution: institutions don't call it a standard of care but rather "hospital policy." Sometimes a psychiatric unit will have its own policy that spells out its procedures for working with suicidal patients. There is a tendency, I think, to argue that not following one's unit's own policy is indefensivle. I do not think that is true. Many policies were written by peple who put *ideal care* in their policy. I have said more than once from the witness stand that the ideal care is not the standard of care. If we could do everything we put down in those policies, we would be doing a tremendous job.

A (Maris): I need to say one thing in response to the comments raised about what I said earlier. I don't know if Mary was, in fact, low-risk. I was not claiming that she was low-risk. I was saying, "How could we account for the treatment that she got?" Some people might superficially look at Mary and say that because we have to account for the fact that standard of care seems so far below standard, so deviating, and so unusual, one way of justifying that would be to see her as somewhat less of a risk. I am not sure whether I think Mary was a high or a low-risk. For example, professionals have a tremendous range of suicide rates. Typically, surgeons have a low risk, and psychiatrists have a high risk. If you look at any occupational category, even within medicine, there are tremendous variations in suicide rates. I think Mary probably had a high risk for suicide. But I am saying it would be easy to give her a little bit more autonomy than was good for her. Never forget we know that Mary killed herself. That is something we know only in hindsight. What if you had this case without the ending? Would you have then predicted that Mary would be a suicide?

A (Perlin): It has simply not been my experience that by-laws speak to "ideal care." The by-laws may be antiquated. Perhaps no one has reviewed and revised the by-laws in quite some time. But in cases that I have reviewed in hospitals, by-laws certainly must be considered. If there exists a policy on your particular unit, I think it is wise to know to what degree that policy agrees or differs from the written by-laws. If it differes, I suggest that at the least you should try to revise the by-laws in accordance with the policy you want on the ward. My point simply is that it is appropriate to know what your own written rules and regulatiosn are. Not to know them, it seems to me, is to carry an unnecessary added risk.

A (Litman): There are two points that I want to emphasize, since this is really a teaching/learning case conference. I want to emphasize the aspects of taking notes. "Standard of care" has wide margins, but it does include taking notes on what you are doing. Second, I want to emphasize that Mary is a very valuable person. If this goes to trial, and the hospital loses, the hospital will be viewed as having very deep pockets. We are talking about seven figures. She's a professional, a young mother with great earning power, and so on. So those two things are very much in the minds of the attorneys. I'd like to shift our attention from Dr. Smith to the responsibility of Dr. Jones. In my own practice I have had occasion to raise concerns about another psychiatrist's practice. I feel that if there were clear concerns on the part of Dr. Jones at the hospital, there should have been more consistent follow-up in referring Mary back to Dr. Smith. What was the expected outcome of that, and in what way could Mary have been redirected if returning to Dr. Smith was not considered the prudent way for her to continue her treatment? She was not happy and not really getting anything out of therapy. Why not refer her to a different person or change her direction in some way? No one seems really to be concerned with the role of the hospital because she obviously improved while at the hospital. Something did go right for her; and then she was sent directly back to the person who had not helped her in the past and who did not show a lot of concern or willingness to help her while she was at the hospital.

A (Litman): That is a well-made point. That is why, originally, the plaintiff's lawyer will sue everybody in a very wide net, to capture all of those records and all of those reports. The notes in the hospital record—they are required to have notes there—will indicate a lot about how much they took this to heart. We know that Dr. Jones was worried. Now the question is, did he do the right thing according to a standard—did he do what a prudent and competent psychiatrist would do when he faced the feeling that his colleague, Smith, was not doing the right thing? Did Jones do enough, and did he do the right thing? There would be a strategy battle among the lawyers here. If Smith has a lot of insurance, some lawyers would be tempted to let Jones off the hook in order to have him testify against Smith. These are strategy battles. But Jones, as you say, may have neglected to do something because he was impressed by Smith. We would have to find out. Jones may have been negligent.

Q: Just a comment. It is hard for me to believe this case could be so badly managed. I wonder if that wasn't a function of Mary's being treated in her own institution, where she gets caught up in all of the professional rivalries, staff conflicts, turf issues, and all of the problems of a staff member being a patient. I wonder, for example, if Smith was angry at a junior physician for not doing what she was supposed to be doing. Any and all of the personal/professional relationships would have disturbed the therapy. It might have been wiser to have sent her to a different facility for treatment, where she could be simply a patient. A staff physician gets treated with special kinds of consideration. Often people who should be patients, doctors or celebrities, are not treated as patients. She obviously did not get good treatment.

Q: I have been trying to find a source of references as to the actual incidence of malpractice suits again psychiatrists and psychologists, civil actions charging malpractice in the assessment and treatment of suicide cases. Is there an available data base?

A (from audience): I know that the American Psychological Association (APA) keeps records through their insurance trust of actions against psychologists. The National Association of Social Workers also has ongoing records. Although social workers are rarely sued, the practice is increasing.

A (from audience): The same is true of the American Psychiatric Association (APA). The insurance committee of the APA gives a report every year on all suits that were brought and defended by the APA policy. If the defendants used other policies, the APA would not have that information. But that is one nationwide source of data that they would be happy to share.

A (Litman): We know several things. The number of suits are increasing, and the scope of the net that is cast is widening. When Farberow and I did a study of suicide in psychiatric hospitals (Litman & Farberow, 1966) (this has been confirmed in recent surveys, too), we found that about 1% of the suicides, about 300 a year, occur in hospitals. Nowadays nearly all of those are followed by some sort of a suit, and often there is some sort of monetary settlement. Suits against outpatient therapists used to be very rare. An outpatient therapist had to do something egregiously wrong, but that too is changing. More and more there are suits for a mix-up in drugs, prescribing the "wrong" drugs, or taking the "wrong" approach. In this particular case there are mutliple causes for complaint. Anybody who does not keep notes on what he or she is doing is close to malpracticing because this practice can be detrimental to the patient.

A: I work in a setting totally separated from a clinic, hospital, or mental health center type of setting. The people who work in the programs under my management and supervision are spread all over the United States. None of those people is a psychiatrist. Most of them are not psychologists; most of them are not MSWs, nurses, or other professional personnel. Most of them are paraprofessionals, untrained individuals in roles in which they are assessing and in some cases diagnosing cases for which they have questionable abilities. I am very concerned about that. I constantly warn them about legal ramifications, liability, malpractice and so on. Yet because of a lack of other services or personnel in the areas they work in—for example, in the U.S. Army's Community Services program—it is very difficult for some of them to say, "I can't handle this." Rather than say no, they take on these cases. I would like to hear your thoughts about such people assessing, diagnosing, treating, referring, and otherwise managing patients.

A (Litman): Many persons are at risk of being caught in the net of lawsuits; for example, intake workers in a halfway house, school counselors, teachers, and so on, but each person is judged by this mythical "standard" that says that what you do has to be reasonable and prudent according to your place, your training, and your occupation. For example, in all of the years I directed the Los Angeles Suicide Prevention Center, we had telephone counselors working on a suicide prevention hotline. We have never had a lawsuit, although we often had 100 different counselors, with only 8 weeks of training and minimal to medium supervision, handling all sorts of things. We had a definite mortality by suicide; 1% of our clients are dead by suicide at the end of 2 years according to three different follow-up studies. But never a lawsuit. Why? I would be glad to defend anything we did except possibly a wide breach of our own rules. That is what we could not defend. We have a rule, for instance, that counselors are not to go out into the field to people's homes and visit them there. If one of our counselors were to do that, we might be vulnerable to a lawsuit if, as a result, somebody did commit suicide in association with the rule violation. Occasionally, we have had fearful things happen when people broke the rules and acted unprofessionally; we would have been vulnerable if someone had been damaged. As long as people follow the rules and do what they are supposed to do, they are not vulnerable. For example, suppose one of our counselors gave wrong advice on the telephone; somebody called and said, "I took a bunch of pills," and the counselor said, "Well, you are going to be okay," and the person was not okay. That is probably within the standard of what you can expect from a crisis counselor. They are not really expected to know the lethality of all of the different pills. At any rate, no lawyer has taken such a case. The same thing would go for all paraprofessionals engaged in service delivery. They are expected to function only at their own levels. It is very important to have consultation, supervision, and training, however.

A (Perlin): It is very costly to be defended; even in terms of a frivolous suit. As a result, as a personal decision I will not serve on the board of an organization (e.g., the Samaritans) if it does not have liability insurance. I think I have an obligation to my family to make certain that the service I render, even in a voluntary situation, does not deprive or threaten them in any particular way. At one time I simply assumed certain things, but now I make certain that those considerations are taken care of by liability insurance.

A (Maris): I went to Europe under the auspices of the U.S. Army to talk to military personnel about suicide prevention. I spent the better part of a summer going around looking at the problem of military suicide. I know that the army is concerned about these issues. I have never had a military suicide legal case, but there have been many that could come up, for example, people who do or do not get promoted. In one case I was consulting on in Germany, a man had falsified his Vietnam War record and was demoted from a technical sergeant's rank and had to go back and live in the barracks with the soldiers he had been training. I have never consulted on such a suit.

Q: Have any of you ever been involved in or hear of a situation in which a suit is brought for the treatment of a suicidal individual in which there were no untoward effects on the individual, that is, there was no suicide or no subsequent suicide attempt? Most of our concerns are about the deaths that occur or the serious attempts and sequelae. In other areas of medicine and in our clinical practice one can be sued for almost any issue; but the treatment of a suicidal individual involves a variety of methods; and if we are successful in the treatment, we don't see the untoward effect. We have actually prevented something. Have you ever experienced or heard of a situation regarding a suit relating to the quality of treatments received?

A (Litman): Yes. In all degrees, there are all different kinds of suits. Corresponding to what this question raises would be when a patient says it was a waste of time: "I lost my money; nothing happened"; "I was promised a cure; my treatment was fraudulent." But that would not necessarily be alleging malpractice. It would just be fraud and a waste of time. There have been instances like that. To charge malpractice, however, and to collect, there has to be an injury. The physician has to have done something or failed to do something (commission or omission) that either caused or aggravated the injury. Of course, there are other types of suits—sexual involvement, false arrest, false imprisonment, and for divorce and custody—in which a psychiatrist has been involved, and the person who has lost has sued the psychiatrist.

A (from audience): The most frequent type of suit brought against psychologists is a "fee dispute" case, in which the patient has failed to pay the therapist's fee, has been dunned, and sued the therapist in return. Suits alleging sexual behavior between therapist and patient are, I think, next most frequent. Suicide is somewhat further down the line in the hiearchy of court actions brought against psychologists.

Q: About malpractice suits against volunteers or paraprofessionals, in some states there are "Good Samaritan Acts" that cover all individuals who work as volunteers for a suicide crisis hotline or any kind of practice. Even on the road, if you find someone injured, as long as the act of intervention has been done with good intent, you cannot be held liable for loss of life or even injury that may result. With regard to volunteers evaluating medication, as Dr. Litman indicated, in practice volunteers and staff of suicide crisis hotlines do not give medical advice of any kind. To do so is a breach of policy of these centers. If a volunteer that I knew of did that, he or she would be immediately dismissed. We refer to poison control or we refer to hospital emergency rooms for any type of medical advice.

A (Litman): You do not and will not get in trouble when you follow policy. The problems arise when somebody fails to get the message. Not only are there frivolous suits, there are many suits that are malicious. I think as experts we have an obligation to discourage such lawsuits. I think that this problem is getting much worse. Of the many I have refused to be involved in, I did so because the plaintiffs or their attorneys were actually creating something that was not there. Sometimes mental health workers try their best with a very difficult chronic-suicidal situation, and often their thanks, if somebody dies, is a lawsuit. You start to ask yourself why anybody would work with these chronic high-risk-for-suicide patients. They are very difficult people, and sometimes suicides happen. I feel great sympathy for mental health workers who have to deal with these patients. Somebody has to deal with them, even though those that do may end up getting sued.

A (Perlin): In the context of malpractice, on a more sophisticated level, we can learn to provide better treatment as a consequence of malpractice suits. I have learned four things, keeping in mind that I am mostly involved in suits following or related to hospital discharge. First, as Dr. Litman has already mentioned, keep notes, and in those notes, document your assessment of suicide risk. In my experience, it is not uncommon for people who keep notes—when the person is depressed, for example—to not ask about suicide. It is not enough to make a note about depression. Second, I find it just extraordinary how many therapists seem to go on vacation immediately following discharge of a suicidal patient. Obviously, I am not saying we should not have vacations. In these cases the vacationing therapists were covered by another doctor. Whether the other doctor knew anything or a lot about the case is really not so much the issue; the appropriate clinical advice is to have the patient *seen* by somebody on follow-up, not simply given a name. A recently discharged patient should, in my view, see a clinician for several weeks after discharge. Third, in four of eight cases I recently reviewed, I noted a very odd phenomenon, which I am seeing more and more; namely, at the point of discharge, the dosages of prescribed drugs are decreased. The psychiatrist apparently does not want the patient to go home on or with as much medication as was given in the hospital at the time of transition. The last point, which I think is terribly important, is that when someone on the ward asks about suicidal ideation and "no suicidal ideation" is recorded in response to the question, as in the case of Mary, what often is overlooked is the existence of a delusion. The last case I reviewed involved a very similar woman who was fearful that she would kill her child. In the hospital she became more organized, was not "suicidal" according to the usual inquiry, but committed suicide to prevent herself from harming the child. Indeed, there are studies that conclude that delusional patients may be more at risk. But in many instances we do not ask about a delusion, which may be more contributory to the act of suicide, and that may be a significant omission on the part of the caregiver.

REFERENCES

Berman A.L. (1986, August). *Suicide as malpractice issue.* Paper presented at meeting of the American Psychological Association, Washington, DC.

Berman, A. L., & Cohen-Sandler, R. (1983). Suicide and malpractice: Expert testimony and the standard of care. *Professional Psychology: Research and Practice, 14,* 6–19.

Chemtob, C. M. Hamada, R. S., Bauer, G., Kinney, B., & Torigoe, R. Y. (1988). Patients' suicides: Frequency and impact on psychiatrists. *American Journal of Psychiatry, 145,* 224–228.

Chemtob, C. M., Hamada, R. S., Bauer, G., Torigoe, R. Y., & Kinney, B. (1988). Patient suicide: Frequency and impact on psychologists. *Professional Psychology: Research and Practice, 19,* 416–420.

Coser, R. L. (1976). Suicide and the relational system: A case study in a mental hospital. *Journal of Health and Social Behavior, 17,* 318–327.

Goldstein, R. L. (1987). The psychiatrist's role in retrospective determination of suicides: An uncertain science. *Journal of Forensic Sciences, 32,* 489–495.

Holmes, T. H., & Rahe, R. H. (1967). The social adjustment rating scale. *Journal of Psychosomatic Research, 11,* 213–218.

Kobler, A. L., & Stotland, M. (1964). *The end of hope.* New York: Free Press.

Litman, R. E., & Farberow, N. L. (1966). The hospital's obligation toward suicide prone patients. *Hospitals, 40,* 64–68.

Mack, J. (1988, April). *The conditions of collective suicide and the threat of nuclear war.* Paper presented at the annual meeting of the American Association of Suicidology, Washington, DC.

Maris, R. W. (1981). *Pathways to suicide: A survey of self-destructive behaviors.* Baltimore: The Johns Hopkins University Press.

Pope, K. (1986). Assessment and management of suicidal risk. *The Independent Practitioner, 6,* 17–23.

Pope, K. (1989). Malpractice suits, licensing disciplinary actions and ethics cases: Frequencies, causes and costs. *The Independent Practitioner, 9,* 22–26.

Smith, K. (1985). Suicide assessment: An ego vulnerabilities approach. *Bulletin of the Menninger Clinic, 49,* 489-499.

Epilogue

- Thirty thousand suicides each year.
- Five hundred thousand nonfatal attempts each year.
- An inestimable number of individuals who consider the possibility of suicide, some maintaining a preoccupation with that goal at the level of obsession but held back from acting by a countercathexis sufficiently strong to maintain just enough of a difference for now.

These individuals, singly and together, command our attention to the commentaries in this volume, the specific proposals made, and the insights precipitated by the contributors' suggestions and responses.

Suicide prevention has become a national priority. As evidence of this, the U.S. Department of Health and Human Services' 4-volume *Report of the Secretary's Task Force on Youth Suicide* (Alcohol, Drug Abuse, and Mental Health Administration, 1989) presents 50 commissioned papers and makes recommendations based on the work of three major task forces convened in middecade to deal specifically with the alarming rise in the incidence of youth suicide. In addition, the U.S. Public Health Service has drafted their "Year 2000 Objectives for the Nation" (U.S. Department of Health and Human Services, 1989) to promote health and prevent disease. Signficiant among these objectives is a reduction in the rate of suicide in the United States. The Public Health Service has proposed, furthermore, to dramatically increase the proportion of professionals trained in the early identification of those at risk. Corrollary objectives in the areas of substance abuse, depression, and gun safety have the potential to make a measurable impact on rates of suicide among defined groups as well.

What is inherent in these federal initiatives is a stated commitment to doing something about the problem of suicide versus a longer-held strategy of benign neglect. What are absent from these public health objectives are specific recommendations designed to accomplish them and, as yet, the financial investment necessary to support them. The current effort parallels a similar Public Health Service report at the beginning of the 1980s that established measurable targets to be reached by 1990, objectives that have not been met. Federal priorities tend to shift with the political winds and the crises of tomorrow. It is yet to be seen whether there now will be a sustained and supported commitment to something more than cheerleading the promotion of our national health and the prevention of premature mortality.

What should be apparent to the reader of this volume is a consistent tone of optimisim about suicide prevention. Each contributor has expressed a "can do" philosophy, suggesting many "somethings" that can be done to make a positive impact on the lives of suicidal individuals and on the incidence of suicide. In some instances—for example, in the cases of suicide landmarks (jumping sites) and clusters (chapters 1 and 2)—the total number of individuals potentially affected is small, perhaps no more than 5% of annually determined suicides. But the themes presented in the contributors' discussions have generalizability well beyond the numbers of suicides circumscribed by the case material. Were a similar focus applied to gun safety measures, particularly where youth suicide is concerned, and/or to the effective monitoring of abusable prescription drugs so readily available to the suicidal individual, the impact on large numbers of people would be considerable.

Additionally, these chapters present a common focus on the issue of exposure and consequent, possibly imitative, events, particularly as covered by the media. Elsewhere, I have summarized what is known (and not known) about these effects and have recommended interventive strategies of potential impact (Berman, 1989).

The discussions presented in Part I of this volume have several other common themes that should serve as foundations to our thinking about suicide prevention. Iterated throughout are foci of (1) the need for cooperative efforts between various segments of the community (mental health and the schools, the media, etc.); (2) the need for liaison, consultation, and support between caregivers and colleagues; (3) the need for anticipatory considerations, programmatic policies and procedures in place and ready to be implemented before, rather than after, the problem crisis occurs; and (4) the need to maintain a preventive awareness of the needs of survivors, who become new at-risk individuals if not so considered.

The discussions in Part II, centering on more idiopathic and clinical considerations, share quite similar themes: (1) the need to consider treatment as involving more than strictly clinical foci (e.g., the law, ethics, etc.); (2) the need for consultation and support; (3) the need for appropriate risk assessment and a diagnostic focus, as well as the treatment choices available and tailored to the individual case presentation; and (4) the need to involve potential survivors in one's treatment considerations.

Only six cases were chosen for this volume. Given that the potential range of such cases is quite broad, it is encouraging that such consistent themes were derived. Perhaps that is one of the values of problem-oriented case methods of instruction: the learning derived goes well beyond the specifics posed by the idiosyncrasies of the case and speaks to some core of teachable principles.

The overriding statement made in these commentaries is that we can and should be active in our efforts to prevent suicide, whether on a community-wide or individual level. The "we" in that statement is instructive. Suicide prevention is not the business of the other guy; it is not strictly an issue for the mental health community. Suicide is a public health problem and therefore the business of all segments of society. In the end, if we are to make a difference, all of us must consider ourselves suicidologists.

REFERENCES

Alcohol, Drug Abuse, and Mental Health Administration. (1989). *Report of the Secretary's Task Force on Youth Suicide (Volumes 1–4)*. DHHS Pub. No. (ADM 89-1624. Washington, DC: U.S. Government Printing Office.

Berman, A. L. (1989). Interventions in the media and entertainment sectors to prevent suicide. In Alcohol, Drug Abuse, and Mental Health Administration. *Report of the Secretary's Task Force on Youth Suicide: Volume 4. Strategies for the prevention of youth suicide* (pp. 186–194). DHHS Pub. No. (ADM) 89-1624. Washington, DC: U.S. Government Printing Office.

U.S. Department of Health and Human Services, Public Health Service. (September, 1989). *Promoting health/preventing disease: Year 2000 objectives for the nation*. (Draft for public review and comment).

Index